Third Party Releases by Means of Bankruptcy Law Guarantees and (Mass) Tort

Third Party Releases by Means of Bankruptcy Law Guarantees and (Mass) Tort

Lindsey Simon, Ralph Brubaker, Riz Mokal,
Sid Pepels and Ruud Hermans

Nederlandse Vereniging voor Rechtsvergelijkend en Internationaal Insolventierecht (NVRII) / Netherlands Association for Comparative and International Insolvency Law (NACIIL)

eleven

Published, sold and distributed by Eleven
P.O. Box 85576
2508 CG The Hague
The Netherlands
Tel.: +31 70 33 070 33
Fax: +31 70 33 070 30
e-mail: sales@elevenpub.nl
www.elevenpub.com

Sold and distributed in USA and Canada
Independent Publishers Group
814 N. Franklin Street
Chicago, IL 60610, USA
Order Placement: +1 800 888 4741
Fax: +1 312 337 5985
orders@ipgbook.com
www.ipgbook.com

Eleven is an imprint of Boom (Den Haag).

ISBN 978-90-4730-168-4
ISBN 978-94-0011-325-1 (E-book)

Preface

Can bankruptcy law offer debt relief to third parties that are not themselves involved in a formal procedure? This question is explored both as to guarantees and as to mass tort liability. These questions have been the main topic of controverse in the US, in cases such as Purdue Pharma and the opioid crisis. Taken together, the answer to these questions will be decisive as to the future scope of bankruptcy law and its relation to other fields of law.

The following reports have been made available by the following authors.

Lindsey Simon (University of Georgia School of Law). She has firmly put the use of US Chapter 11 as an instrument for solvent defendants on the map in her seminal article Yale Law Review article '*Bankruptcy Grifters*'.[1] She describes the phenomenon that bankruptcy grifters latch onto the debtor, using bankruptcy's special devices like channeling injunctions and third party releases to force claimants into settlements that threaten procedural justice. Her work also provided the initial inspiration for the theme of the annual meeting 2022 of NACIIL. At the annual meeting of NACIIL, Simon presented her ground breaking research culminating in her Yale Law Review article with updates. For inclusion in our NACIIL series, she provided us with a high level analysis of the phenomenon of bankruptcy grifters and her key research findings, entitled '*Mass Tort Reckoning: The Ongoing Influence of Bankruptcy Grifters in the United States*'.

Ralph Brubaker (University of Illinois College of Law). He wrote the report '*Third-Party Nondebtor Releases for "Bankruptcy Grifters": A Response to Professor Simon*'. Brubaker and Simon both agree that 'bankruptcy grifting' it is a very significant systemic problem. The views of Simon and Brubaker do differ as to what to do about it. Brubaker his position is very clear where he argues that there should be a flat prohibition on nonconsensual nondebtor releases.

Riz Mokal (Barrister, South Square, London) provided an English perspective and many contributions to the policy debate in his report entitled. 'Third Party Releases in English Restructuring Law: Pragmatism and Propriety'. Most fascinating is the use of third party liability as part of the English reorganization landscape. Whereas liability is normally a position most like to escape from, it can also be assumed in order to restructure by means of so-called deed polls. This provides a prime example of English ingenuity in the field of reorganization.

1 See L. Simon, *Bankruptcy Grifters*, 131 Yale L. J. 1154 (2022). There is also a free online version available, that can be accessed on ssrn via https://papers.ssrn.com/sol3/papers.cfm?abstract_id=3817530.

Sid Pepels (Radboud University & Jones Day) wrote a report entitled: '*Third Party Releases under WHOA: a warm welcome for a very limited number of guests only?*'. Given the very recent enactment of the WHOA in January 2021, there is very little case law still. Pepels explores the potential of the WHOA and discusses what its scope and boundaries should be both as to group guarantees and other forms of third party liability.

Ruud Hermans (Judge and former De Brauw Blackstone Westbroek and professor at Radboud University) wrote a report entitled: '*Settling Mass Damage Claims Inside and Outside Insolvency Procedures: A Comparison of the Available Procedures*'. Herein he compares the possibilities and pitfall of dealing with mass tort liability under collective redress and insolvency law. In his opinion, in order to protect the interests of the injured parties, it will be necessary, and unavoidable, that either the legislature or the judiciary will set limits on what is allowed as to using which procedure.

The annual meeting took place at the University of Amsterdam on June 16, 2022. This year, annual meeting also formed the celebration of the 10 year anniversary of NACIIL. We celebrated in the beautiful courtyard of the Oudemanhuispoort, University of Amsterdam with a (moon)walking dinner.

On behalf of the board of NACIIL 2022-2023

Rolef de Weijs (chair)

Table of contents

Mass Tort Reckoning: The Ongoing Influence of Bankruptcy Grifters in the United States

Lindsey D. Simon[*]

At its 2022 annual meeting, the Netherlands Association for Comparative and International Insolvency Law (NACIIL) brought together a panel of international experts to discuss how third party releases impact the claim resolution process in bankruptcy.[1] Besides engaging in debates with the other speakers, I presented my research on the topic culminating in my article *Bankruptcy Grifters*, 131 Yale L. J. 1154 (2022).[2] The following is a high level overview of both the topic of bankruptcy grifters as well as the contributions from my research.

My analyses focus on a phenomenon central to many mass tort bankruptcies in the United States: defendants who seek third party releases to resolve claims against them in a chapter 11 case without actually filing for bankruptcy. To understand why this is appealing to well-financed companies, one must first put into context the US landscape for mass tort litigation outside of bankruptcy. Formal aggregate litigation in the United States primarily takes place in the form of multidistrict litigation ('MDLs'), a consolidation scheme designed to collect federal cases before one court for pretrial matters but return them to the original court for final adjudication. Although the class action device was a commonly utilized approach to resolve mass torts in the past, Supreme Court precedent has narrowed the possibility of obtaining class certification[3] and limited what relief a class action may offer for universal peace.[4] MDLs are notoriously costly and slow, and defendants involved in them cannot expect to resolve all claims – even if they reach a settlement with an overwhelming majority of claimants. When facing thousands of lawsuits in courts across the country, it is no surprise that companies are drawn to any strategic alternative. Enter bankruptcy.

---

* Robert Cotten Alston Associate Chair in Corporate Law, University of Georgia School of Law.

1 NACIIL annual meeting, 'Third Party Releases by Means of Bankruptcy Law', June 16, 2022, Amsterdam.

2 There is also a free online version available, that can be accessed on ssrn via https://papers.ssrn.com/sol3/papers.cfm?abstract_id=3817530.

3 *See* Abbe R. Gluck & Elizabeth Chamblee Burch, *MDL Revolution*, 96 N.Y.U. L. Rev. 1 (2021) (outlining the pushback on class actions and shift to MDLs).

4 Linda S. Mullenix, *The Short Unhappy Life of the Negotiation Class*, 56 Michigan Journal of Law Reform (April 1, 2022).

My original article, *Bankruptcy Grifters*, 131 Yale L. J. 1154 (2022) was the first to examine the prevalence of 'bankruptcy grifters', parasitic entities that attach to a host debtor, taking many benefits of the bankruptcy process but paying few of its costs. Bankruptcy offers many appealing features to US debtors. First, the automatic stay pauses all litigation and collection efforts against the debtor in any other setting (court or otherwise). Second, bankruptcy consolidates all pending cases into one forum before one judge, a feature even the MDL process cannot mandate (as it only reaches federal and not state court cases). These two features give debtors time and space to negotiate, a precious commodity when litigation overshadows a business' ability to operate. Finally, bankruptcy provides the debtor with a complete and binding determination of all claims through confirmation of a plan of reorganization. This, too, is a significant advantage over nonbankruptcy aggregate litigation, which currently cannot bind future claims or individuals who did not get the chance to opt out or otherwise consent.

Yet all of the special protections that Congress designed to help debtors successfully reorganize come with steep costs. Beyond the vast monetary expense, debtors in the United States must expose themselves to scrutiny and transparency in the bankruptcy process, including mandatory disclosures of company financials, deposition-like interviews, and more. Although debtors receive some deference for decisions involving company management, court oversight is integral to maintaining the balance between a reorganizing debtor and its creditors. The bankruptcy system requires debtors to seek review and approval for many actions that would otherwise be completely discretionary. This review – by design – invites stakeholders like creditors and a federal watchdog agency to appear and be heard on the debtor's actions while in bankruptcy.

Despite bankruptcy's benefits, many financially burdened companies will not become debtors. Some do not file to avoid the cost, disclosure, and oversight that debtors must endure. Other companies that want to file for bankruptcy may not be eligible. Recent court decisions indicate that companies without sufficient financial distress may have their cases dismissed for bad faith.[5] Clever companies (bankruptcy grifters) have recognized ways to seek the consolidation and settlement benefits of bankruptcy without actually filing for bankruptcy. Bankruptcy grifters latch onto the debtor, using bankruptcy's special devices like channeling injunctions and third party releases to force claimants into settlements that threaten procedural justice.

Releases and channeling injunctions are two procedural mechanisms in the Bankruptcy Code that effectively require all identified claims to pursue recovery against a trust instead of the released party. The idea was originally used to address current and future litigation challenges in asbestos cases – such as *Johns-Manville* – through reliance on the bankruptcy court's § 105(a) powers. Congress later codified into § 524(g) what the parties and courts had created and expressly provided guidelines for non-

5 In re: LTL Management LLC, No. 22-2003 (3d Cir. 2023).

debtor channeling injunctions in asbestos cases. Congress did not, however, address the possibility of such injunctions (and the releases that go along with them) in cases involving other types of mass torts. The silence on this point lies at the core of current debates over third party relief.

Circuits are split on the availability of releases and channeling injunctions for nondebtor entities when claimants do not consent. In the jurisdictions where nonconsensual third party releases are available, they are commonly granted to directors, officers, agents, insurers, distributors, affiliates, product sellers, and simple codefendants. As Professor Brubaker and others have identified,[6] without express direction from Congress in the Bankruptcy Code, third party releases should face both jurisdictional and constitutional challenges. Indeed, these arguments have gained momentum in recent years as district courts in the *Purdue Pharma* bankruptcy and other cases rejected plans with third party releases.[7] But while the appellate process unfolds in various circuits, mass tort defendants continue their pursuit of relief in chapter 11. What began decades ago as a narrow solution for asbestos bankruptcies has expanded to a degree that is inconsistent with the bankruptcy system's limited scope.

Bankruptcy courts have emboldened new-era bankruptcy grifters by allowing difficult cases to broaden the scope of nondebtor relief. Current trends involve companies attempting to shift mass tort liability to subsidiaries or newly created entities, which then file for bankruptcy. The solvent parent offers to fund a litigation trust, all in exchange for a channeling injunction and nondebtor release. These bankruptcy grifters have become even more emboldened, stretching the boundaries of corporate law to create a debtor with expansive litigation exposure, only to use that debtor to obtain universal peace for the parent.[8] So far, defendants are willing to risk failure; even obtaining the benefit of the automatic stay (and preliminary injunctions, for nondebtors) is a valuable outcome if the case ultimately gets dismissed. In mass tort litigation, time is quite literally money. To date, these cases seem limited only by attorneys' creativity, their clients' willingness to fund it, and, of course, the bankruptcy courts' oversight.

These cases pose grave concerns, both regarding the integrity of the bankruptcy system (is this really what Congress intended?) and the procedural gauntlet claimants face (what rights are being lost?). To analyze them properly, and to offer a path forward, it was first critical to understand what is actually happening on the ground, both strategically and factually. Each case is different, but trends and patterns emerge that show not only the common features of a mass tort bankruptcy trust but also outlier elements that should be either championed or prohibited. One of the most important contribu-

---

6 Ralph Brubaker, *Mandatory Aggregation of Mass Tort Litigation in Bankruptcy*, 131 Yale L.J.F. 960 (2022).

7 Decision and Order on Appeal at 7, In re Purdue Pharma L.P., No. 21-cv-08566-CM (S.D.N.Y. December 16, 2021).

8 *See, e.g.*, In re: LTL Management LLC, No. 22-2003 (3d Cir. 2023) (describing how Johnson & Johnson created LTL Management LLC through the so-called "Texas Two-Step").

tions of my research is a comprehensive discussion of the ways that debtors set up trusts to restrict or expand a tort claimant's rights in bankruptcy.

After tracing the progression of bankruptcy grifters in chapter 11 cases – including pending bankruptcies from the opioid epidemic and sex abuse scandals – the research breaks new ground by proposing specific procedural and substantive limitations that protect claimants and deter grifting behavior. By explaining how nondebtors grift on chapter 11 cases and identifying the ways that channeling injunctions and releases redirect litigation away from solvent entities, the research sets the foundation for assessing current mass tort cases. It looks past current practice into the future, assessing which changes could make the most difference, and the best way to go about it – through Congress or the courts. Congress has pending draft legislation to nearly eliminate third party releases, yet the likelihood of success seems remote. Appellate courts may rule on the issue at various points in the near future, but until the Supreme Court decides the matter, debtors will undertake a venue shuffle to find courts open to granting the relief. For now, judges must narrow the benefit that bankruptcy grifters receive and provide a careful assessment of the path they leave for claimants to recover.

In the United States, bankruptcy is a valuable forum designed to resolve difficult problems. Under the proper circumstances and with appropriate safeguards, bankruptcy may ultimately be an important system in which defendants and claimants address mass tort liability. Instead of eliminating third party releases and completely blocking the viability of mass tort bankruptcy, stakeholders on all sides should continue to scrutinize this important issue, analyze individual cases, and step in where possible to prevent claimants from losing critical procedural rights.

Third-Party Nondebtor Releases for "Bankruptcy Grifters": A Response to Professor Simon

Ralph Brubaker[*]

1. Introduction

It is a great honor to participate in this celebration of the tenth anniversary of the Netherlands Association of Comparative and International Insolvency Law. Prof. Dr. Rolef de Weijs is to be congratulated for choosing such a timely and fascinating topic for this year's program: third-party (or nondebtor) releases.

I have been writing about third-party releases for the past 25 years, and I have been one of the most persistent and vocal critics of the practice. Nondebtor-release practice is receiving considerable renewed attention in the U.S. now because of a number of very high-profile mass-tort bankruptcies, such as the Boy Scouts of America, USA Gymnastics, and various Catholic diocese cases (all involving large-scale sexual abuse claims) and the Purdue Pharma and Mallinckrodt opioid cases. In each of those cases, various nondebtor parties have used or are using the bankruptcy filing of a corporate debtor to try to have their own liability, for their own alleged misconduct, discharged, by making whatever the bankruptcy court ultimately signs off on as a sufficiently "substantial" contribution to a settlement fund.

That practice is receiving very critical coverage in the popular press, and legislation has been introduced in the U.S. Congress that would prohibit nonconsensual nondebtor releases. In addition, there was a very dramatic and sensational development in December 2021 in the *Purdue Pharma* case. Purdue, which was owned and managed by the Sackler family, manufactured the opioid OxyContin. The bankruptcy court presiding over Purdue's reorganization proceedings confirmed a plan of reorganization in September 2021 that released the Sacklers from any personal liability to opioid claimants, in exchange for their multibillion-dollar contribution to a settlement fund.[1] On appeal,

---

* James H.M. Sprayregen Professor of Law, University of Illinois. This Report is an edited and annotated version of remarks I delivered at the 2021/2022 annual meeting of the Netherlands Association of Comparative and International Insolvency Law (NACIIL) in Amsterdam on June 16, 2022. I thank NACIIL and Prof. Dr. Rolef de Weijs for the invitation to participate, and I thank all of the presenters and participants at that conference for their extremely insightful and informative comments and conversations.

1 *In re Purdue Pharma L.P.*, 633 B.R. 53 (Bankr. S.D.N.Y. 2021).

though, a federal district court in New York vacated the confirmation order and, at least temporarily, blew that deal up, holding that the bankruptcy court had no authority to approve the liability releases for the Sacklers.[2] That decision has been further appealed to the Second Circuit Court of Appeals, which has heard oral argument, but has not yet issued a decision. Regardless of how the Second Circuit rules, though, many expect the case to go up to the U.S. Supreme Court, because there is a long-standing disagreement in the lower court as to whether nondebtor releases are permissible (outside of the kinds of asbestos cases in which the U.S. bankruptcy statute explicitly authorizes some kinds of nondebtor releases).

My article excerpted in the NACIIL meeting materials[3] is a response to Professor Lindsey Simon's "Bankruptcy Grifters" article in the *Yale Law Journal*.[4] There is no disagreement between Simon and me about whether bankruptcy grifting is a good or a bad development, in general. We both agree that it is a very significant systemic problem. Our only disagreement is what to do about it.

We also agree regarding the pivotal end-game relief that makes bankruptcy grifting possible, which is so-called nonconsensual third-party or nondebtor "releases" and channeling injunctions that give nondebtor defendants, who have not filed bankruptcy themselves, the equivalent of a discharge from all of their mass-tort liability. That nondebtor discharge is accomplished through the so-called "release" approved by the bankruptcy court, which parallels the debt discharge that a bankruptcy debtor receives through the bankruptcy process, complete with a permanent injunction prohibiting the mass-tort plaintiffs from thereafter suing the released nondebtors. That nondebtor discharge effectively forces the mass-tort plaintiffs to pursue their claims solely through the bankruptcy process, against a settlement pot comprised of the bankruptcy debtor's assets that go into the settlement pot, plus amounts paid by the released nondebtors into the settlement pot in exchange for their "releases."

Simon is of the view that nondebtor-release practice is so entrenched at this point that it is futile to try to prohibit it. In addition, she does not seem to be convinced that an outright prohibition on nonconsensual nondebtor releases is appropriate. Thus, she proposes helpful reforms to nondebtor-release practice.

My Response to Simon's proposed reforms pushes at both of the premises for those proposals, because I hold a more extreme view of nondebtor-release practice. As a normative policy matter, I believe there should be a flat prohibition on nonconsensual nondebtor releases, which is the view I articulated in a book-length law review article 25 years ago,[5] and I believe that subsequent developments have made the case for a flat

2 *In re Purdue Pharma, L.P.*, 635 B.R. 26 (S.D.N.Y. 2021).

3 Ralph Brubaker, *Mandatory Aggregation of Mass Tort Litigation in Bankruptcy*, 131 Yale L.J.F. 960 (2022).

4 Lindsey D. Simon, *Bankruptcy Grifters*, 131 Yale L.J. 960 (2022).

5 Ralph Brubaker, *Bankruptcy Injunctions and Complex Litigation: A Critical Reappraisal of Non-Debtor Releases in Chapter 11 Reorganizations*, 1997 U. Ill. L. Rev. 959 (1997).

prohibition even stronger. I have also not given up on the feasibility of a flat prohibition. On that score, and somewhat ironically, all of the renewed attention that nondebtor releases are receiving (which Simon's *Bankruptcy Grifters* article has actually helped fuel) may well increase the chances that the U.S. Supreme Court will finally take up the issue and decide whether nonconsensual nondebtor releases are permissible under existing law.[6]

I have discussed that legality question elsewhere and at length.[7] For the purposes of this discussion, then, I want to focus on the normative policy question and why I believe there should be a flat prohibition on nonconsensual nondebtor releases. First, though, I need to provide some contextual background, starting with a basic taxonomy of the various kinds of bankruptcy releases. A brief description of resolution of mass torts outside of bankruptcy is also in order, because it makes clear why nonconsensual nondebtor releases are so controversial and, in my opinion, normatively indefensible.

2. UNCONTROVERSIAL NONDEBTOR RELEASES

To set the stage for my discussion of the most controversial kinds of releases (and injunctions that implement them), it is helpful to distinguish them from those releases and implementing injunctions that are not at all controversial.

There is clearly authority for the bankruptcy estate's representative, be it a trustee or Chapter 11 debtor-in-possession, or even a creditors' committee if authorized to pursue claims on behalf of the estate, to compromise claims and causes of action belonging to the estate and give the defendants a release of those settled claims. The bankruptcy court can approve those settlements, and the U.S. bankruptcy statute expressly provides that the terms of such a settlement can be incorporated into a debtor's plan of reorganization.[8]

That kind of settlement and corresponding release of claims belonging to the bankruptcy estate includes causes of action that individual creditors or shareholders could

6 Indeed, I think it is highly likely that all of the public furor over nondebtor releases contributed to the New York district court's ruling in the *Purdue Pharma* case, cited and discussed *supra* note 2 and accompanying text, in which the court took a fresh look at the nondebtor-release practice that has taken hold over the past 30 years, and ultimately came to the conclusion (which I believe is correct) that nondebtor-release practice is not only extremely troubling but also illegitimate and unlawful. That was a very shocking decision that few (if any) anticipated, not least because that same judge had said exactly the opposite in a different case only a few years earlier: that nonconsensual nondebtor releases are permissible. *See In re Kirwan Offices S.à.R.L.*, 592 B.R. 489, 511 (S.D.N.Y. 2018), *aff'd*, 792 F. App'x 99 (2d Cir. 2019).

7 *See, e.g.*, Brubaker, *supra* note 3, at 966-986; Brubaker, *supra* note 5, at 1028-1080; Ralph Brubaker, *Nondebtor Releases and Injunctions in Chapter 11: Revisiting Jurisdictional Precepts and the Forgotten* Callaway v. Benton *Case*, 72 Am. Bankr. L.J. 1 (1998) [hereinafter Brubaker, *Nondebtor Release Jurisdiction*].

8 11 U.S.C. § 1123(b)(3)(A); *see Protective Comm. for Indep. Stockholders of TMT Trailer Ferry, Inc. v. Anderson*, 390 U.S. 414 (1968).

pursue outside bankruptcy. For example, fraudulent conveyance claims are claims assertable by individual judgment creditors outside bankruptcy. When the debtor who allegedly made a fraudulent transfer files bankruptcy, however, the U.S. bankruptcy statute gives those state-law fraudulent transfer claims to the debtor's bankruptcy estate to pursue on behalf of all creditors.[9] A bankruptcy filing, therefore, preempts individual creditors' fraudulent conveyance claims, which are stayed once the debtor files bankruptcy, and the estate representative thereafter has exclusive authority to prosecute and (with bankruptcy-court approval) settle that cause of action.[10]

The same is true for corporate derivative suits that individual shareholders could prosecute outside bankruptcy, for example, against corporate officers and directors for breach of their fiduciary duties. Once the corporation files bankruptcy, though, that cause of action belongs to the estate; any nonbankruptcy suit on it is stayed; and the bankruptcy process determines the fate of that cause of action.[11]

Another uncontroversial category of releases, which is very similar to the one just discussed, are those releases that prevent individual creditors from pursuing or interfering with the estate's property rights, for example, the estate's insurance policies that provide proceeds to cover claims against the debtor. There are various and sundry nonbankruptcy state laws that permit individual claimants whose claims are covered by insurance to bypass the insured and seek to collect insurance proceeds directly from the insurer. Liability insurance policies and their proceeds, however, are property of the estate when the insured files bankruptcy, so individual creditors' suits and other actions that attempt to recover policy proceeds from the insurer are stayed.

Moreover, to fund a plan of reorganization, a Chapter 11 debtor-in-possession may strike a deal with the insurance company to simply pay out the policy limits to the estate. And, of course, the estate's corresponding commitment in that settlement is to fully release the insurer from any further claims under the policy, which is property of the estate. Indeed, that was the court's rationale in the seminal 1988 decision approving the insurance injunction in the Johns-Manville massive asbestos-liability bankruptcy.[12] Such insurance injunctions are clearly permissible and should not be at all controversial.

There is a very similar *in rem* property-of-the-estate rationale for injunctions protecting purchasers in a bankruptcy sale of the debtor's business from creditors' claims for successor liability and for injunctions protecting individual partners from creditor

9 11 U.S.C. § 544(b)(1).

10 *See* Charles Jordan Tabb, Law of Bankruptcy § 3.6, at 259 (5th ed. 2020).

11 *See* Ralph Brubaker, *The Fundamental (and Limiting) Status Quo Function of Bankruptcy's Automatic Stay*, 41 Bankr. L. Letter No. 2, at 1, 9 (February 2021).

12 *See In re Johns-Manville Corp.*, 843 F.2d 636 (2d Cir. 1988); *see generally* Ralph Brubaker, *Supreme Court Validates "Clarified"* Manville *Insurance Injunction: Channeling … and So Much More!*, 29 Bankr. L. Letter No. 8, at 1 (August 2009).

claims of personal liability for partnership debts in the bankruptcy proceedings of the partnership.[13] Also relatively uncontroversial are injunctions protecting defendants who settle with the estate against later claims for indemnity or contribution by non-settling codefendants.[14]

The *only* nondebtor, third-party claims for which releases are controversial are *direct* claims by individual creditors or shareholders against a nondebtor third party for that nondebtor's own conduct that gives rise to a cause of action belonging to those individual creditors or shareholders. A common example of such a direct claim by an individual creditor or shareholder is an allegation that certain individuals within the debtor corporation or in other entities (such as affiliates, insurers, or other creditors) personally participated in fraud or other tortious misconduct that injured the creditor or shareholder and that gives that creditor or shareholder a cause of action directly against that tortfeasor for their own tortious conduct.

That tort cause of action does not belong to the debtor's bankruptcy estate; it belongs to the individual creditor or shareholder personally. Consequently, the debtor's estate and its fiduciary representatives have no authority whatsoever to prosecute that cause of action belonging to the individual creditor or shareholder (rather than the estate).[15] Ergo, the debtor's estate and its fiduciary representatives also have no authority to compromise that claim belonging to the individual creditor or shareholder.

With respect to those kinds of direct third-party nondebtor claims, the bankruptcy court clearly has some injunctive powers. For example, the U.S. Supreme Court has held that a bankruptcy court has the power to temporarily stay the prosecution of third-party nondebtor claims in order to facilitate an orderly and expeditious reorganization for the debtor.[16] In addition, all courts seem to agree that if an individual creditor or shareholder consents to a release or compromise of its third-party nondebtor claim, then the bankruptcy court can approve that consensual release.[17]

---

13 *See* Brubaker, *supra* note 5, at 962 n.3.

14 *See, e.g.*, *In re Munford, Inc.*, 97 F.3d 449 (11th Cir. 1996); *see generally* Ralph Brubaker, *An Incipient Backlash Against Nondebtor Releases? (Part I): The "Necessary to Reorganization" Fallacy*, 42 Bankr. L. Letter No. 2, at 1 (February 2022).

15 *See Caplin v. Marine Midland Grace Trust Co.*, 406 U.S. 416 (1972).

16 *See Celotex Corp. v. Edwards*, 514 U.S. 300 (1995); *see generally* Brubaker, *Nondebtor Release Jurisdiction*, *supra* note 7, at 22-47, 59.

17 The only bone of contention is what action (or inaction) by a creditor or shareholder is a sufficient indication of consent to the release. For example, is doing nothing to affirmatively opt out of a proposed release properly considered consent to that release? If the necessary consent is given, though, binding a creditor or shareholder to a settlement and release to which the creditor or shareholder has freely consented is also not at all controversial. *See, e.g.*, *In re Specialty Equip. Cos.*, 3 F.3d 1043, 1045-1047 (7th Cir. 1993).

3. Nonconsensual Nondebtor Releases

The *only* controversial "releases," then, are nonconsensual nondebtor releases of creditors' and shareholders' *direct* third-party nondebtor claims that bind all creditors and shareholders, whether they have consented or not, and even over their express objections, the same way the debtor's bankruptcy discharge binds all creditors and shareholders with respect to their claims against and interests in the debtor. Why are those releases so controversial? And why do I think a flat prohibition on nonconsensual nondebtor releases is the better response to the bankruptcy grifter problem from a normative policy perspective?

In thinking about those questions, it is important to recognize that the distribution and discharge scheme for nondebtors that is effectuated via nonconsensual nondebtor releases departs from bankruptcy norms for distribution and discharge in all sorts of ways, like allowing released individuals to discharge debts for fraud or intentional torts and punitive damages that they could not discharge if they were to actually file bankruptcy. And remedying some of the most significant departures from bankruptcy norms seems to be the principal objective of Simon's proposed reforms.

Even more importantly, though, given that released nondebtors have *not* filed bankruptcy and that many (if not most or even all) of them could not or would never even consider actually filing bankruptcy, not least because many are eminently solvent notwithstanding their mass-tort exposure, nonconsensual nondebtor releases also violate fundamental, immutable *nonbankruptcy* norms for effectuating aggregate settlements of mass-tort liability.

Consider, for example, plaintiffs' mass-tort claims against a solvent nondebtor, such as a codefendant with the debtor who is an alleged joint tortfeasor, or even a *principal* tortfeasor on torts for which the corporate debtor, as employer/principal, is only *vicariously* liable for the tortious conduct of the corporation's employees/agents. What nonconsensual nondebtor releases allow such a released nondebtor to do is impose a mandatory no-opt-outs settlement of the nondebtor's mass-tort liability on all plaintiffs, whether they all agree to the settlement or not.

Note in particular, then, that the mandatory settlement that nondebtor releases impose on nonconsenting plaintiffs is, necessarily, a settlement negotiated and agreed to by someone else – that is, someone other than the claimants on whom the settlement is imposed. Thus, it is a kind of representational settlement, like a class action, and those kinds of representative litigation and settlement processes have the potential to violate individual claimants' most fundamental substantive and procedural rights, in all sorts of ways. Those rights are preserved and protected in the United States via the due process guarantees enshrined in the U.S. Constitution. And the U.S. Supreme Court has an extensive jurisprudence on the constitutional due process rights of individual claimants, in order for such a representational settlement process to be valid. Most significantly, there is a long line of decisions regarding the right of individual claimants to "opt out" of the representative process (at least for the kinds of damages claims that are settled via nonconsensual nondebtor release) and pursue their individual claims on their own.[18]

The normative policy question that poses is this: given that there is no permissible nonbankruptcy process for a solvent defendant[19] to impose a mandatory no-opt-outs settlement of its mass-tort liability on claimants, why should there be such a process only when a codefendant has filed bankruptcy? There must be something about *the debtor's* bankruptcy filing that justifies having a mandatory no-opt-outs settlement process for these claims (against *a nondebtor*) that does not and cannot exist in the absence of the debtor's bankruptcy filing.

The standard justification that is given is that the nondebtor-release settlement is "necessary" or "essential" to successful reorganization of the debtor. And, of course, one of the distinctive and prominent policy justifications for having a Chapter 11 corporate reorganization process is an overt policy and preference in favor of reorganizing operating businesses, rather than shutting them down and liquidating them. Not only may reorganization bring more aggregate value to the debtor's creditors, but it can also produce various collateral benefits, for example, to the employees of the business who keep their jobs, for the communities in which the business operates, etc. *If* a mandatory nondebtor-release settlement were, in fact, necessary to keep a debtor's business operating, then that could supply a compelling normative justification for a mandatory no-opt-outs settlement of a nondebtor's mass-tort liability to claimants. Indeed, the most critical stated requisite, as formulated by the courts, is that a nonconsensual nondebtor release can be approved only to the extent it is necessary or essential to the debtor's successful reorganization.

As applied by the courts, though, that "necessity" standard (that I have elsewhere dubbed the "necessity" fiction[20]) does *not* mean that if nonconsensual nondebtor releases were prohibited and simply unavailable, the debtor would have to shut down its business and liquidate. As applied, it merely means the nonconsensual nondebtor release is necessary or essential to the complex series of compromises embedded in the proposed plan of reorganization. In other words, the "necessity" case is (always): "Your honor, the nonconsensual nondebtor release is necessary to do this particular deal, and if you do not approve the release, this deal will fall apart."

But *all* Chapter 11 reorganizations involve a series of compromises over any number of things. That is what Chapter 11 is – a structured negotiation framework. Consequently, if nonconsensual nondebtor release deals are permissible, and if the necessary to "reorganization" standard for approval is nothing more than necessary to "do the

18 *See* Ralph Brubaker, *Assessing the Legitimacy of the "Texas Two-Step" Mass-Tort Bankruptcy*, 42 Bankr. L. Letter No. 8, at 1, 8-9 (August 2022).

19 And perhaps even for an insolvent defendant. *See id.*

20 *See* Brubaker, *supra* note 3, at 986-992.

deal," then that is a nonstandard. It is simply a negotiating script for nondebtors. The predictable negotiating position of nondebtors who have something to contribute that the debtor's bankruptcy estate and its representatives want, like a large contribution to a settlement fund for payment of mass-tort claimants, will be: "Look, a nonconsensual nondebtor release is an absolute deal-breaker condition for me to contribute anything. The only way we can do a deal is if I get a nonconsensual release of all my mass-tort exposure."

"Necessary to reorganization," then, because it means nothing more than necessary to do this deal, does not supply any unique bankruptcy justification at all for allowing nondebtors to impose a mandatory no-opt-outs settlement on nonconsenting claimants. It is just a negotiating position that says nothing about the ability to successfully reorganize the debtor if nonconsensual nondebtor releases were prohibited and unavailable. It supplies no legitimate justification for permitting a mandatory no-opt-outs settlement of a nondebtor's mass-tort liability *only* when a codefendant has filed bankruptcy.

4. Conclusion

If mandatory no-opt-outs settlement of solvent defendants' mass-tort liability is a good idea, then it should be available as a matter of nonbankruptcy law. And that reasoning, of course, is a classic "creditors' bargain" approach to this problem. Indeed, the bankruptcy grifter phenomenon that Simon documents is a vindication of at least one aspect of creditors' bargain theory, which predicts that if we dramatically change parties' substantive rights in bankruptcy, the inevitable result will be forum shopping, whereby parties opt for the bankruptcy forum *solely* to take advantage of the rule change in bankruptcy and *not* because there is a good bankruptcy reason for sorting out the parties' rights in bankruptcy.[21] And that kind of forum shopping into bankruptcy seems to be precisely what we are now witnessing with mass-tort litigation and the bankruptcy grifter phenomenon – a migration of mass-tort litigation against nondebtor codefendants out of the tort system and into the bankruptcy system, because the bankruptcy system is the only place where those codefendants can impose a mandatory no-opt-outs settlement of their mass-tort liability on nonconsenting plaintiffs.

21 *See* Thomas H. Jackson, The Logic and Limits of Bankruptcy, Harvard Univ. Press, Cambridge, Mass, 21-27, 33, 45-46, 193-201 (1986); Douglas G. Baird & Thomas H. Jackson, *Corporate Reorganizations and the Treatment of Diverse Ownership Interests: A Comment on Adequate Protection of Secured Creditors in Bankruptcy*, 51 U. Chi. L. Rev. 97, 100-101, 103-104 (1984).

Third-Party Releases in English Restructuring Law

Pragmatism and Propriety

Riz Mokal[*]

1. Introduction

The United Kingdom ('**UK**') and the United States ('**US**') are divided not only by a common language but also by their approach to the release of third party rights. Focusing on England and Wales,[1] restructuring law is immensely powerful. It consists mostly of judge-made principles woven densely around a sparse statutory skeleton. It openly permits the use of a very wide range of legal manoeuvres and artificial structures intended to forum-shop in favour of English restructuring law and practice. In particular, it permits debtors who may or may not be distressed ('**the real debtor**') to create a new entity ('**the nominal debtor**') that can unilaterally take on co-obligations in relation to pre-existing liabilities and to propose a restructuring of those liabilities that, if approved, discharge the real debtor. Unlike the US, however, the affected creditors are necessarily entitled to vote on the restructuring. Crucially, English law vests immense discretion in the English court, with the attendant strengths and weaknesses. Amongst other things, the court may reject a restructuring that has obtained the requisite statutory majority support from creditors. However, the level of scrutiny and scepticism with which the restructuring is assessed depends on the presiding judge and on the existence and extent of active opposition to the restructuring.

Aimed at a non-UK readership and focusing on doctrinal detail, this paper introduces English restructurings undertaken by way of schemes of arrangement ('**schemes**') and restructuring plans ('**RPs**' or '**plans**') pursuant to Parts 26 and 26A of the UK Companies Act 2006[2] insofar as they may be designed to obtain third-party releases. In the US, such releases have caused very significant concern in the context of the restructuring of mass tort liability. While such restructuring is very rare in England, the paper examines the recent case of *Amigo*, concluded in May 2022, which involved financial

---

* Barrister, South Square, London; Honorary Professor in Laws, University College London; Honorary Research Fellow, Aberdeen University School of Law; email: rizmokal@southsquare.com. The views expressed here, the mistaken ones in particular, are mine alone.

1 With no disrespect intended to Wales, I will refer to this jurisdiction as England. Scotland and Northern Ireland have relevantly similar but less frequently used restructuring laws.

2 Company voluntary arrangements are not considered.

mis-selling claims, as a case study. This case shows the importance of active opposition to a proposed restructuring and, inevitably in a discretion-heavy system, the identity of the judge presiding over the process. The paper concludes by highlighting some of the differences with US law and practice.

2. How to Release Third Party Claims in English Law

The primary differences between the scheme and RP proceedings are that (i) RPs are only available to companies in "*financial difficulties*", whereas there is no entry threshold for schemes,[3] (ii) RPs have a powerful cross-class cram-down mechanism that is lacking in the scheme (though there are ways, in use since at least the late Victorian age, in which a partially equivalent effect can be achieved),[4] and (iii) there is no 'numerosity' requirement in the RP, as explained below. None of these differences is relevant to this paper and is not considered further.

2.1 Origins

The lineage of the scheme can be traced to the first statutory composition in English law.[5] A composition is essentially an arrangement between a debtor and two or more of the debtor's creditors by which the debtor obtains some remission or postponement of his obligations to them.

The first statutory composition was introduced by a 1696 statute, An Act for Relief of Creditors, by Making Compositions with their Debtors, in case Two-Thirds in Number and Value Do Agree. It applied to natural persons rather than to companies, at a time when the corporate form was not widely available. The process was not successful

3 For academic discussion, see Riz Mokal, 'The Difficulties with "Financial Difficulties": The Threshold Conditions for the New Pt 26A Process' (2020) 10 *Butterworths Journal of International Banking and Financial Law* 662-664. For judicial consideration, see *Re gategroup Guarantee Ltd* [2021] BCC 549 (Ch), [177]-[179] (Zacaroli J). The present author was part of the counsel team for the company proposing the RP in *gategroup* but writes here exclusively in his personal capacity. The views expressed here must not be attributed to the company or its legal advisors.

4 For academic discussion, see Riz Mokal, 'The Two Conditions for the Part 26A Cram Down' (2020) 11 *Butterworths Journal of International Banking and Financial Law* 730-733, and 'The Court's Discretion in relation to the Part 26A Cram Down' (2021) 1 *Butterworths Journal of International Banking and Financial Law* 12-16. There is now very extensive and ever-growing judicial treatment of the UK cross-class cram down mechanism. For interesting case studies, see Christian Pilkington and Will Stoner, *Pilkington on Creditor Schemes of Arrangement and Restructuring Plans* (3rd ed, London: Sweet & Maxwell, 2022), Annexes 4, 5, 10, and 11.

5 This section draws on Sections 3.3 and 3.4 of Riz Mokal, 'What is an Insolvency Proceeding? *Gategroup* Lands in a Gated Community' (2022) 31(3) *International Insolvency Review* 1-56. https://doi.org/10.1002/iir.1470 (hereafter, 'Mokal, "Insolvency Proceeding"').

and was repealed the subsequent year. A somewhat different version of the composition was reintroduced by the 1825 Act to Amend the Laws relating to Bankruptcy, and other versions were enacted in legislation in 1842, 1844, and 1849. The 1861 Bankruptcy Act has been described as a "'breakthrough' *in providing a workable debtor-in-possession composition mechanism*".[6]

These variants of the statutory composition differed as to the type of debtor who could propose them (whether the debtor had to be a "*trader*" or alternatively could be anyone irrespective of whether they could be characterised as a trader), the legal status of the debtor (whether they were or were not subject to the statutory bankruptcy process), the intended purpose of the process (as a substitute to or means for the liquidation of the debtor's assets in order to pay creditors), the extent of the court's involvement (whether one or more hearings were required as part of the process), and the creditor majorities required for a successful vote (which varied from three-fifths in number and value of those present and voting to nine-tenths in number or in value of all creditors holding claims worth more than a statutory threshold).

The first *corporate* composition was introduced by the Companies Act 1862, enacted the year after the introduction of the "*breakthrough*" version of the composition for natural person debtors. This statute, which is recognised as the direct progenitor of the current Scheme process,[7] permitted a company which was about to be or in the course of being wound up to propose an arrangement to its creditors which would be binding on creditors if approved by 75% by number and value of creditors who were present and voting at a meeting called for this purpose.

The scheme process subsequently developed in three important respects. First, the Joint Stock Companies Arrangements Act 1870 permitted "*any compromise or arrangement*" proposed between a company in winding-up and its creditors or any class of them to be put to a vote of creditors. If approved by a majority in number representing three-quarters in value and sanctioned by the court, the "*arrangement or compromise*" would be binding on all creditors or all members of the relevant class of creditors. Second, the Companies Act 1900 first introduced the power for such "*compromise or arrangement*" also to be put to the company's member or any class of members. And third, the Companies Act 1907 removed the necessity for the company to be in winding-up.

The scheme process has remained materially unaltered since that time. Subject to the three differences noted above, the same principles and process also carry through to the RP process, introduced by the Corporate Insolvency and Governance Act 2020, which inserted the new Part 26A into the Act.

---

6 Mokal, "Insolvency Proceeding", p. 23.

7 See for example Jennifer Payne, *Schemes of Arrangement: Theory, Structure and Operation* (2nd ed) (Cambridge University Press, Cambridge, 2021), p. 6.

2.2 Sources

The legal principles governing the scheme and RP processes derive from three sources.

The first source is statute. The statute only provides the bare bones of the process: the current version, found in Parts 26 (scheme) and 26A (RP) of the Act, contain just eight and eleven sections (respectively), most of which are very brief. In particular, these provisions confer jurisdiction on the court to convene one or more meetings of the relevant classes of stakeholders, require an explanatory statement ('**Explan**') and certain notices to be provided to such stakeholders, set out the majorities that a scheme or plan must obtain in the relevant stakeholder class(es), confers jurisdiction upon the court to sanction a scheme or plan which has obtained the requisite majorities, and where the scheme or plan is intended to facilitate or bring about a reconstruction or amalgamation of the company, empowers the court to make provision for certain matters (such as the transfer of the company's business, and the allotment or appropriation of shares, debentures, or policies, etc.).

The second source of the legal principles governing the scheme and RP processes is the jurisprudence of the court developed since the 1860s. This provides the bulk of guidance as to the process, including as to the nature of the "*compromise or arrangement*" that may be put to creditors and/or members, the nature of the information to be provided to them, the proper constitution of stakeholder classes, and the factors to be considered by the court in deciding whether to call a meeting of the relevant stakeholders and whether to sanction a scheme which has attained the relevant statutory majorities.

As for the RP, much of the body of principles developed in case law in relation to the scheme also apply to the RP, and some of the principles stated in the rapidly expanding RP jurisprudence are also relevant to the scheme.

The third source is the '**Practice Statement**' issued by the Chancellor of the High Court. The current version was issued on 26 June 2020. The Practice Statement crystallises the principles derived from case law, and acquires authority as a statement of such guiding principles by virtue of being expressly approved and applied in the judgments of the English courts. It is "*to be applied except in so far as in the circumstances of the particular case the party objecting to its application shows that it would be wrong in principle to do so*".[8] It provides guidance on several key aspects of the scheme and RP processes.

8 *Brook v Reed* [2012] 1 WLR 419 (Court of Appeal of England & Wales) at 431, [48] (David Richards J, as he then was, addressing a different practice statement but by dicta which are equally applicable here).

2.3 *Process Overview*

The scheme and RP processes characteristically operate in four stages. The first is an informal pre-statutory stage ('**Informal Stage**'), while the remaining three ('**Convening Stage**', '**Voting Stage**', and '**Sanction Stage**') are governed by the Act and by the principles deriving from the other sources we have identified above. I will consider these stages in turn.

2.4 *Informal Stage*

Before the formal, court-based process is launched, the company or (where the company is in formal insolvency proceedings) its insolvency officeholder will invariably engage with key stakeholders in order to explore their appetite for a restructuring; identify sources of new funding; formulate preliminary proposals for a restructuring of relevant classes of its liabilities, its equity, and/or its operations; negotiate with key stakeholders in order to develop and refine the restructuring proposal; and seek maximal buy-in from members of the relevant stakeholder constituencies, including (where practicable) through legally binding 'lock-in', 'lock-up', or 'restructuring support' agreements. Often, this will be linked to other 'backstop' arrangements which serve to ensure that a central stakeholder group would provide financial support if a wider stakeholder class were to fail to do so.

2.5 *Convening Stage*

The formal scheme or RP process commences with an application ('**the convening application**') to the court for an order to convene one or more meetings of the relevant stakeholder classes. This application may be made by the company, any of its creditors or members, its liquidator (if it is being wound up), or its administrator (if it is in administration, an insolvency proceeding subject to the UK's Insolvency Act 1986).[9] In practice, virtually all such applications are made by the company or, occasionally, by the company's insolvency officeholder.

Prior to the hearing of the convening application, and unless there are good reasons for not doing so,[10] the applicant should take all reasonable steps to notify any person affected by the scheme – through what has come to be known as the '**Practice State-**

9 Sections 896 (scheme) and 901C (RP) of the Act. As noted, both also permit an application by a creditor or shareholder of the debtor company.

10 In practice, the only such reason is very pressing urgency, and this rarely applies.

ment Letter' – that the scheme is being promoted, the purpose which the scheme is designed to achieve, and the proposed class composition. The notification should (at least in theory) be in a concise form. Notice should be given in sufficient time to enable those affected by the scheme to consider what is proposed, to take appropriate advice and, if so advised, to attend the hearing of the convening application ('**the convening hearing**'). What is adequate notice will depend on all the circumstances. The evidence at the convening hearing should explain the steps which have been taken to give the notification and what, if any, response the applicant has had to the notification.[11]

At the convening hearing, the applicant should draw to the attention of the court any issues relating to the following matters (amongst others).[12]

The first such issues relates to the constitution of classes. A class must be confined to those persons whose rights are not so dissimilar as to make it impossible for them to consult together with a view to their common interest.[13] This principle has two implications. Firstly, those whose rights really are so dissimilar that they cannot consult together with a view to a common interest should be treated as if they are parties to different arrangements and should be placed into separate classes. Secondly, those whose rights are sufficiently similar to the rights of others that they can properly consult together should be required to do so, lest by ordering separate meetings the court gives a veto to a minority group.[14] What matters is the similarity or dissimilarity of rights (not interests), and of rights against the company (not against third parties). Rights are compared in two scenarios: (i) in the absence of a scheme or plan, often referred to as "*the comparator*", and (ii) if the scheme or plan were successfully implemented.

The second issue is the fundamental one of whether the court has jurisdiction to sanction the scheme or plan. Five sub-issues issues are generally relevant here. Firstly, the court would have to be satisfied that the company is a "*company*" within the meaning of the Act.[15] Secondly, the court must have *in personam* jurisdiction over the company. This may arise because the company is incorporated or registered in England or has its centre of main interest there or else chooses to submit to the court's jurisdiction. Thirdly, the court must have subject matter jurisdiction in relation to the scheme or plan, which it would have if there is a "*sufficient connection*" with England.[16] This can include the existence of English law governed agreements. Fourthly, the scheme or plan must constitute a "*compromise or arrangement*". This has been given a broad interpretation. All that is required is some element of give and take, as opposed to mere surrender

11 See paragraphs 7-8 of the Practice Statement.
12 Pursuant to paragraph 6 of the Practice Statement.
13 *Sovereign Life Assurance v Dodd* [1892] 2 QB 573, 583; *Re UDL Holdings Ltd* [2002] 1 HKC 172, 179 (Lord Millett NPJ).
14 *Re Hawk Insurance Company Ltd* [2002] BCC 300, [33] (Chadwick LJ).
15 Sections 895(2) (scheme) and 901A(4) (RP) of the Act.
16 *In re Drax Holdings Ltd* [2004] 1 WLR 1049, 1055, [29] (Lawrence Collins J).

or forfeiture.[17] Fifthly, the scheme or plan must be between the company and the relevant classes of its stakeholders in their capacity as such.[18]

The third issue encompasses all other matters not going to the merits or fairness of the scheme or plan, but which might lead the court to refuse to sanction it. Here, the court is concerned with whether there is what was traditionally described as a "blot" on the scheme and more recently as a "*fundamental roadblock*"[19] or "*show stopper*".[20] This would be a problem not going to the court's jurisdiction which is nevertheless so egregious that the court can foresee that it would not be able to sanction the scheme or plan even if approved by the relevant stakeholders. That the proposed scheme/plan would, if sanctioned or implemented, breach a legal obligation is an example of such a show stopper, but there are other issues that may be so categorised.[21]

If a person fails to raise an issue referred to above at the convening hearing and seeks to raise the issue at the second hearing ('**the sanction hearing**', discussed below), the court will "*expect them to show good reason why they did not raise the issue at an earlier stage*".[22]

The court also assesses the adequacy of the Explan[23] and, if not satisfied, may refuse to convene the statutory meeting(s) sought by the convening application. The Explan should be in a form and style appropriate to the circumstances of the case, including the nature of the relevant stakeholders, and should be as concise as practicable. It should explain the commercial impact of the scheme/plan and should provide stakeholders with such information as is reasonably necessary to enable them to make an informed decision as to whether or not the scheme or plan is in their interests, and on how to vote on it. The court does not, however, approve the Explan, whose adequacy may yet be challenged at the sanction hearing.[24]

If the court is satisfied on all these matters, it will make an order for the convening of one or more meetings of the relevant stakeholder classes in such manner as the court directs.[25]

The court does not at this stage consider the merits or fairness of the proposed scheme/plan, which will arise for consideration at the sanction hearing if the scheme or plan is approved by the statutory majority.[26]

---

17 See *Re Savoy Hotel Ltd* [1981] Ch 351 (Nourse J), 359D–F; *Re Lehman Brothers International (Europe) (in admin.)* [2018] EWHC 1980 (Ch); [2019] BCC 115 (Hildyard J), [64].
18 *In re Lehman Brothers International (Europe)* [2010] Bus LR 489 (CA), [65]-[67].
19 *Re Indah Kiat BV* [2016] BCC 418, 426, [28].
20 *Re The Royal London Mutual Insurance Society Ltd* [2018] EWHC 2215 (Ch), [10].
21 *In re T & N Ltd (No. 4)* [2006] EWHC 1447 (Ch), [19].
22 Paragraph 10 of the Practice Statement.
23 Which must be sent to all relevant stakeholders; sections 897 (scheme) and 901D (RP) of the Act.
24 Paragraphs 14-15 of the Practice Statement.
25 Sections 896(1) (scheme) and 901C(1) of the Act.
26 *Re Telewest Communications plc* [2004] BCC 342, [14] (David Richards J).

2.6 *Voting Stage*

The second formal stage of the scheme and RP processes consists of the meetings of the relevant stakeholder classes. The scheme is approved by the relevant stakeholder class if, in the meeting of that class, a majority by number representing 75% in value of the members of the class present and voting agree the comprise or arrangement.[27] The requirement that a majority in number of the members of each relevant class vote in favour of the scheme is the numerosity requirement to which I referred above. There is no equivalent numerosity requirement in the RP, so that a class is deemed to have voted in favour of the RP if at least 75% by value of the members of the class so vote.[28]

2.7 *Sanction Stage*

The third formal stage consists of the sanction hearing.[29] At this hearing, the court considers the following matters in particular.[30]

First, the court must consider whether the provisions of the statute have been complied with. The key issues here are generally whether the stakeholder classes were properly constituted for the purposes of voting (if there is a challenge on this point), whether meetings were summoned and convened properly in accordance with the convening order, and whether the statutory majorities were obtained.

Second, the court must consider whether each class was fairly represented by the meeting, and whether the majority was coercing the minority in order to promote interests which are adverse to the class that they purported to represent. The primary issue are generally whether some of the stakeholders who voted in favour of the plan did so because they held special interests adverse to those of their class as a whole.[31]

Third, the court must consider whether the scheme or plan was a fair one which a creditor could reasonably approve. There is no absolute rule that the court must accept the verdict of the majority. The court does not act as a rubber stamp. The sanction of a scheme or plan is ultimately a discretionary matter for the court. Where, however, the scheme has been approved by the requisite statutory majority, and the class was fairly represented at the meeting, there is a presumption that the scheme is fair.[32] The court

---

27 Section 899(1) of the Act.

28 Section 901F(1) of the Act.

29 Sections 899 (scheme) and 901F (RP) of the Act.

30 *Re Telewest Communications plc (No. 2)* [2005] BCC 36, [20]-[22] (David Richards J); *Re Noble Group Limited* [2019] BCC 349, 387-8, [17] (Snowden J).

31 *Re Lehman Brothers International (Europe)* [2019] Bus LR 1012, 1039-1045, at [85]-[106].

32 Re English, Scottish, and Australian Chartered Bank [1893] 3 Ch 385 at 409 (Lindley LJ); Re Telewest Communications plc (No. 2) [2005] BCC 36 at [22] (David Richards J).

usually proceeds on the basis that where a scheme has been approved by the statutory majority, that majority is a better judge of its own interests than is the court. However, that presupposes that (a) the members of the class are capable of understanding (i) what is proposed and (ii) the alternatives open to them, and that (b) they have been provided with adequate information as to both these issues. Where any of these presuppositions does not apply, the court will be particularly searching as to the fairness of the scheme, irrespective of the vote.[33]

Fourth, the court must consider whether there is any 'blot' or defect in the scheme or plan. This factor has been considered above, in the context of the convening hearing, but will be considered again at the sanction hearing.

If satisfied on all these counts, the court will issue an order sanctioning the scheme / plan.

The court's sanctioning order has no effect until a copy of it has been delivered to the Registrar of Companies.[34] Once this is done, the scheme goes into force according to that order and to any relevant provisions of the scheme.

The scheme or plan is then binding on the company, its creditors and shareholders – including any who voted against the scheme as well as any who did not vote at all[35] – and on any insolvency officeholder.[36]

In what follows, I put together the building blocks by which a scheme or plan may release (or amend) third party rights.

2.8 *Compromise or Arrangement*

Schemes and RPs require that there be a "*compromise or arrangement*" between the company and its creditors or a class of them. This has been given a broad interpretation. All that is required is some element of give and take, as opposed to mere surrender or forfeiture.[37]

33 *Re All Scheme Ltd* [2021] EWHC 1401 (Ch), [100]-[102] (Miles J).

34 Sections 899 (scheme) and 901F(6)(b) (RP) of the Act.

35 These points are most clearly made in two Scottish judgments (Scots law on this point being materially identical to English law): *Re Scottish Lion Insurance Co Ltd* [2010] BCC 650 (Inner House, Court of Session), [46], and *Premier Oil* [2020] CSOH 30, at [111].

36 Sections 899 (scheme) and 901F(5) of the Act.

37 See *Re Savoy Hotel Ltd* [1981] Ch. 351, per Nourse J at 359D–F; *Re Lehman Brothers International (Europe) (in admin.)* [2018] EWHC 1980 (Ch); [2019] B.C.C. 115, per Hildyard J at [64].

2.9 Creditor

Lindley LJ stated in *Re Midland Coal, Coke & Iron Company*:[38]

> *... the word* 'creditor' *is used in the Act of 1870 in the widest sense, and that it includes all persons having any pecuniary claims against the company. Any other construction would render the Act practically useless.*

David Richards J stated in *Re T&N Ltd*:[39]

> *In my judgment,* 'creditors' *in s 425 is not limited to those persons who would have a provable claim in the winding-up of the company, although it clearly includes all those who would have such a claim. As was submitted by Mr Snowden and other counsel, one of the recognised purposes of s 425 is to encourage arrangements with creditors which avoid liquidation and facilitate the financial rehabilitation of the company ... This suggests that as wide a meaning as possible should be given to* 'creditors' *in the section. Having said that, it is important to bear in mind that s 425 is designed as a mechanism whereby an arrangement may be imposed on dissenting or non-participating members of the class and such a power is not to be construed as extending so as to bind persons who cannot properly be described as* 'creditors' *...*
> *... whatever the precise meaning of a compromise or arrangement, it must be proposed with creditors or members of a company. It is implicit that it must be made with them in their capacity as creditors or members and that it must at least concern their position as creditors or members of the company.*

In *In re Lehman Brothers International (Europe) (in administration) (No 2)*, Patten LJ's views were to identical effect:[40]

> *a* 'creditor' *will consist of anyone who has a monetary claim against the company which, when payable, will constitute a debt. Contingent claims are included for this purpose ... As a matter of ordinary language, a creditor is someone to whom money is owed. The use of this word with that meaning is a long-established and essential part of English company law ... Given that* 'creditor' *is not defined in the legislation, it is inconceivable that Parliament should have used the word in the 2006 Act in any but its literal sense.*

38 [1895] 1 Ch 267, 277.
39 [2005] EWHC 2870 (Ch), [40], [45].
40 [2010] BCC 272 (CA), [59].

2.10 Effect on Third Parties

In *Re T&N Ltd (No 4)*, David Richards J pointed out that "*arrangement*" has a very broad meaning, that "*arrangement*" and "*compromise*" were separate concepts and that an arrangement need not involve a compromise. He noted that the great majority of schemes involving members did not involve a compromise. One such example is a scheme under which a third party acquires the shares in the company whether by transfer of shares or cancellation of existing shares and the issue of new shares. This is an arrangement between the company and its members because it involves a change of membership of the company. As these members schemes demonstrated, the give and take that a scheme must involve:[41]

> *... need not be between the members and the company, but may be between the members and a third party purchaser, with the company's only function being to register the transfer of shares and thereby terminate the existing members' status as members.*

David Richards J stated that "... *an arrangement [is not] necessarily outside the [what is now section 895 of the Act], because its effect is to alter the rights of creditors against another party or because such alteration could be achieved by a scheme of arrangement with that other party.*"[42]

In *In re Lehman Brothers International (Europe)*,[43] Patten LJ emphasised that it is not merely the word *arrangement* in itself that must be interpreted in seeking to pin down the permissible limits of the scheme jurisdiction but the full phrase '*arrangement between a company and its* creditors' that gives the expression '*arrangement*' its '*content and meaning*'. Patten LJ referred to criticism of *Re T&N* but stated that it was '*entirely logical*' for the scheme jurisdiction to extend to scheme creditors' rights of action against third parties '*designed to recover the same loss*' on the basis that the release of such rights "*is merely ancillary to the arrangement between the company and its own creditors*".[44]

Patten LJ then extended the same reasoning to "*the inclusion in the scheme of the release of contractual rights or rights of action against related third parties* ***necessary in order to give effect to the arrangement proposed for the disposition of the debts and liability of the company to its own creditors***".[45]

41 [2006] EWHC 1447 (Ch), [50].
42 [2006] EWHC 1447 (Ch), [53].
43 [2009] EWCA Civ 1161, [61].
44 [2009] EWCA Civ 1161, [63].
45 [2009] EWCA Civ 1161, [65].

This ability to affect third party rights through the scheme (or the RP) process where this is necessary in order to give effect to the arrangement proposed in relation to the company proposing the scheme (or RP) has come to be referred to as '***Lehman* necessity**'.

In *gategroup*, Zacaroli J crystallised the principles applicable to the operation of the *Lehman* necessity doctrine. Relevantly, he stated:[46]

> *Where the alteration of creditors' rights against third parties is both ancillary to the arrangement between the company and its creditors and necessary to ensure the effectiveness of that arrangement, then they will be permitted.*

2.11 *Practical Mechanisms*

A scheme or plan must, in general, contain two practical mechanisms in order to effect a variation of non-assenting creditors and third parties, and, indeed, to enable such third parties to benefit from and enforce covenants to that effect within the scheme or plan. First, the scheme or plan must have a mechanism for the appointment of an attorney on behalf of the creditor to do the things that the scheme or plan obliges them to do. Second, the scheme or plan must contain a covenant by the creditor in favour of the company to release or alter rights as against a third party, which is enforceable by the company against its creditors, including non-assenting creditors, following sanction of the scheme or plan.[47]

2.12 *Artificiality and Forum Shopping*

English restructuring law now firmly accepts the distinction between benign and malign forum shopping. This goes back to Newey J's judgment in *Re Codere Finance (UK) Limited*, in which the Judge started by noting that the case before him was an instance of forum shopping and proceeded to characterise it as '*good forum shopping*':[48]

> *Debtors are seeking to give the English court jurisdiction so that they can take advantage of the scheme jurisdiction available here and which is not widely available, if available at all, elsewhere. Plainly forum shopping can be undesirable. That can potentially be so, for example, where a debtor seeks to move*

46 [2021] BCC 549, 163(4).
47 [2021] BCC 722, [38].
48 [2015] EWHC 1233, [18].

> *his COMI with a view to taking advantage of a more favourable bankruptcy regime and so escaping his debts. In cases such as the present, however, what is being attempted is to achieve a position where resort can be had to the law of a particular jurisdiction, not in order to evade debts but rather with a view to achieving the best possible outcome for creditors. If in those circumstances it is appropriate to speak of forum shopping at all, it must be on the basis that there can sometimes be good forum shopping.*

This distinction has been confirmed by numerous first instance cases. In my view, the distinction is undeniable and undeniably important and may in principled terms be set out as follows:[49]

> *Steps taken to facilitate the assumption of jurisdiction by a court are objectionable if intended or reasonably likely to secure sectional benefits to one or more stakeholder constituencies (say, the debtor's directors and shareholders) but to the detriment or at the expense of one or more categories of claimant (say, trade creditors, employees, or tax authorities) with accrued claims against the debtor that are available in the existing forum.*
>
> *By contrast, forum shopping is legitimate if intended or reasonably likely to maximise the value available for the benefit of all relevant claimants considered together without resulting in prejudice to any class of accrued claim holders. Value might be maximised because of enhanced prospects for the restructuring of the debtor's liabilities and/or operations and thus its survival, or for a going concern sale of its business.*

2.13 Use of Deed Poll

The logic of *Lehman* necessity has been extended to apply to a company that accepts, usually by deed poll, liabilities mirroring the extant liabilities of related companies precisely in order to create a *Lehman* necessity and thereby enable the new company to propose a scheme intended to affect the pre-existing liabilities. The deed poll can operate as an entirely unilateral instrument: NewCo may execute a deed poll under which it accepts liabilities to the creditors of OldCo without any requirement that such creditors give their assent or take any other step.

---

49 R. Mokal, 'Shopping and Scheming, and the Rule in Gibbs' (2017) *South Square Digest* 58, at 62; available at https://southsquare.com/articles/shopping-and-scheming-and-the-rule-in-gibbs/ (accessed on 12 June 2022).

In *Re AI Scheme Ltd*, Norris J warned that the interposition of a new company in pre-existing debt relationships should not be "*a matter of mere artifice [but should have] a solid grounding in commercial necessity*".[50] On the facts, he accepted that the *Lehman* necessity had come into existence upon the interposition of a deed poll company. A similar approach has subsequently been taken in several English cases.

2.14 *Jurisdiction and Discretion*

In *gategroup*, the company proposing the RP "*fully acknowledge[d] the artificial nature of the co-obligor structure*".[51] The key part of the debt ('**Bond Debt**') consisted of Swiss law bonds issued by a Luxembourg company ('**Issuer**') that contained an exclusive jurisdiction clause in favour of the Zurich court. As part of the restructuring, the Issuer moved its centre of main interest ('**COMI**') to England, with the result that the English court had insolvency jurisdiction over it. Further, a new English company ('**RestructureCo**') was incorporated by the Issuer's parent. RestructureCo, which had an English COMI, unilaterally assumed parallel liabilities for the Bond Debt. RestructureCo's only assets consisted of contribution rights from other members of the group, and its only role appeared to be to function as the restructuring vehicle for the debt. Its financial difficulties were entirely self-inflicted and arose from its assumption of liability for the debt to be restructured.

Zacaroli J drew attention to the critical distinction between the English court's jurisdiction, on the one hand, and the court's discretion in deciding whether to exercise that jurisdiction on the other. He held that the artificiality of the structures by which the English court was given jurisdiction did not preclude the court from obtaining jurisdiction but instead went to the exercise of the court's discretion whether to sanction the RP. In deciding whether to exercise its discretion in favour of or against sanction, the court would take all circumstances into account:[52]

> *the looseness of the connection between the subject matter of the scheme and the relationship between the company and its creditors is a matter which goes to the exercise of the discretion to sanction the scheme.*
> *In the context of a plan under Pt 26A, the artificiality of the structure is undoubtedly an issue of direct relevance to the discretion to sanction the plan. It is possible to imagine uses of the co-obligor structure employed in this case that would be wholly objectionable. That might be the case where it unfairly over-*

50 *Re AI Scheme Ltd* [2015] EWHC 1233 (Ch), [26].
51 [2021] BCC 549, 166.
52 [2021] BCC 549, 163(5), [171]-[172], [174].

> *rode legitimate interests of creditors pursuant to the contracts governing their relationship with the primary obligor companies or under the system of law, including relevant principles of insolvency law, which applies to the relationship between them.*
> *Similarly, there may be cases where the attempt to compromise plan creditors' rights against third parties was bound to fail because that compromise would not be recognised in any of the relevant foreign jurisdictions where it mattered....*
> *On the other hand, it is possible to envisage a case where the artificial structure is the only solution to enable a restructuring to be effected, all other possible alternatives having been explored and rejected for one or other reason of law or practicability; where the alternative is a value-destructive liquidation; and where the terms of the restructuring demonstrably benefit the affected creditors. In such a case, there would be a powerful argument that the artificiality of the structure should not prevent the company and its creditors being able to take advantage of the English scheme or plan jurisdiction.*

On the facts, Zacaroli J was satisfied that the artificial structure was justified.[53] He took account of the following factors in particular. First, the group and RestructureCo were in serious financial difficulties, which meant that absent a restructuring, the Bondholders would receive only a fraction of their debts in the inevitable insolvency proceedings.[54] Second, and if the restructuring were permitted, there would a CHF 500 million injection of new money from the group's shareholders.[55] Third, the Bond Debt was held mostly in relatively small individual holdings by retail investors, and the high majority requirement for restructuring the Debt under its own terms made such restructuring unfeasible.[56] Fourth, the English RP proceeding had been chosen for the restructuring after an investigation of Swiss and Luxembourg alternatives and represented "the only route for avoiding an insolvency process of the Group which would be highly damaging for all stakeholders".[57] Fifth, the impact of the restructuring on the Bondholders – a five-year 'amend-and-extend' in return for continued payment of contractual interest, and the waiver of a change of control provision – was minimal.[58] Sixth, Swiss law expert evidence indicated that if the Bond Debt was restructured in English proceedings, then this would be recognised and given effect to in Swiss law, on the bases (among others) that the Issuer's COMI was now in England and that the Bondholders had had the right

53 [2021] BCC 722, [13]-[15].
54 [2021] BCC 722, [16].
55 [2021] BCC 722, [17].
56 [2021] BCC 722, [18].
57 [2021] BCC 722, [19].
58 [2021] BCC 722, [20].

to be heard in the English court and had been duly summoned to and participated in the proceedings.[59]

Zacaroli J also made two points on forum shopping. First, to the extent that the co-obligor structure constituted forum shopping, it was not being used to give the English court jurisdiction over the Issuer, the latter already having moved its COMI to England.[60] And second, the co-obligor structure was being used not to enable the debtor to exploit English restructuring law for its own advantage at the expense of a creditor class but with a view to achieving the best possible outcome for all.[61]

2.15 *Constitutional Protection of Property*

There has to date been no constitutional challenge to third-party releases in England, such as pursuant to Article 1 of the First Protocol to the European Convention on Human Rights. The three stages of the test are well known.[62] The first question is whether there is an interference with the complainant's possessions, interpreted to include the repayment (and perhaps other) rights of creditors.[63] Assuming, plausibly, that the restructuring constitutes such an interference, the second question is whether the interference was in pursuit of a legitimate aim and whether it was in accordance with the conditions provided for by law. Again assuming the aim of a good-faith restructuring to be legitimate and in compliance with the law, the third and final part of the test asks whether a fair balance was struck between the demands of the general interests of the community and the requirements of the protection of the individual's fundamental rights. In other words, was there a reasonable relationship of proportionality between the aim pursued and the interference complained of?

In relation to this final part, it can be anticipated that the English court would more likely than not take an approach similar to that taken by the High Court of Ireland, interpreting the constitutional protection for private property in Articles 40.3 and 43 of the Irish Constitution in cases such as *Re Ballantyne Re PLC*, in which Barniville J held that the court's discretion whether or not to sanction the scheme provided an adequate mechanism for striking the requisite balance[64]

59 [2021] BCC 722, [24]-[26], [31].

60 [2021] BCC 722, [21].

61 [2021] BCC 722, [22].

62 See e.g. *Stockholms Försäkrings-och Skadeståndsjuridik AB v. Sweden* (2004) 39 EHRR 23, [47]-[51]; *Luordo v. Italy* (2005) 41 EHRR 26, [65], [67]-[70].

63 *Pressos Compania Naviera SA v. Belgium* (1995) 21 EHRR 301, 334-5 at [31]-[32]; *Stran Greek Refineries and Stratis Andreadis v. Greece* (1994) 19 EHRR 293, pp. 325-6 at [59]-[62]; *Ambruosi v. Italy* (2002) 35 EHRR 5, [21] and [24]; *Bäck v. Finland* (2005) 40 EHRR 48, [57], read with [19]-[20].

64 [2019] IEHC 407, [130].

> *the requirement to obtain the sanction of the Court for a scheme of arrangement…, which sanction will not be granted if this scheme is unfair, inequitable, improperly coercive or unreasonable…, combined with the requirement for a special majority at the relevant scheme meeting as a precondition for such sanction … represents a fair, reasonable and proportionate balance by the [legislature] of the various potentially competing interests involved in a scheme of arrangement.*

2.16 Note of Caution

This is the basis on which English restructuring law permits third-party releases. It is worth emphasising, however, that almost all relevant law is case law emerging from unopposed first instance decisions. It would take only one strongly reasoned first instance judgment to throw restructuring practice into doubt.

And indeed in *Re Port Finance Investment Limited*, Snowden J, among the most brilliant of Chancery judges and now on the Court of Appeal, appeared (while still sitting at first instance) to strike a note of caution:[65]

> *The cases to which I have referred above show that the English court has been prepared (at least at first instance and without full contrary argument) to hold that there is jurisdiction to sanction a scheme where a (newly formed) English company has voluntarily assumed a liability to creditors of a different company and entered into a co-obligor or contribution deed in favour of that other company.*
>
> *In doing so, the courts appear to have treated Patten LJ's comment in …* Lehman Brothers *that Part 26 can include releases of third parties that are* 'necessary in order to give effect to the arrangement proposed for the disposition of the debts and liabilities of the company to its own creditors', *to be satisfied* **simply by the existence, as a matter of law, of a contingent liability on the part of the scheme company that has been voluntarily undertaken to the third party.** *Questions of the degree of artificiality of the structure, the relative lack of benefit to the scheme company, and the commercial justification for the scheme from the perspective of the third party have been treated as matters going to the exercise of the court's discretion, together with questions such as whether the scheme is an example of 'good forum shopping', whether there is a high level of support for the scheme from scheme creditors, and whether the scheme is likely to be recognised in other jurisdictions.*

65 [72]-[74] (emphasis added).

> *At this convening stage, I do not consider that I need to, or should, express my own view on whether that is a correct approach to the jurisdictional question of whether third party releases can be included in a scheme in a case such as the present.*

3. Amigo – A Case Study

3.1 Background

Amigo Loans Limited ('**Amigo**'), a member of the Amigo group ('**Group**'), is a subprime lender servicing borrowers who cannot obtain credit from mainstream lenders. Its ultimate parent, Amigo Holdings PLC ('**PLC**'), is listed on the London Stock Exchange. Amigo's model is to lend on the guarantee of a third party. Between 2005 and 2021, it entered into an estimated 927,000 individual agreements with 507,144 borrowers and 536,097 guarantors (together, '**customers**').

In early 2021, it had 137,000 customers under then current loans. Running up to 2021, there was a marked increase in customer complaints under financial regulations on the bases, variously, that a loan should not have been made because it was unaffordable and/or because the guarantor could not afford the guarantee. In this case, Financial Conduct Authority ('**FCA**') rules require repayment of interest and costs to the borrower and repayment of any amounts paid under the guarantee to the guarantor, plus interest at 8% per annum from the date that the relevant sums were paid over. The customers entitled to these payments were referred to as '**Redress Creditors**'. As of the end of 2021, Amigo's complaints provision for known and potential claims was £150.9 million. Their complaints were handled by the Financial Ombudsman Service ('**FOS**'), which charges claims handling costs to the financial firm against whom a complaint has been made. Amigo owed FOS £12.5 million.

3.2 Insolvency

Amigo's total realisable assets, including its loan book, stood at £315-325 million, and it had guaranteed inter-company loans on which about £324 million was outstanding as at the end of 2020. Therefore, it was insolvent. The costs of an insolvent administration were estimated at £37 million. In the result, neither creditors nor shareholders were expected to receive anything in such a proceeding.

3.3 The Original Proposal

The Group's controllers devised a scheme. In early January 2021, a company was incorporated ('**SchemeCo**') and a fortnight later assumed joint liability alongside Amigo, PLC, and other entities for the liabilities owed by Amigo to Redress Creditors and the FOS, both categories of claimant thereby becoming '**Scheme Creditors**'. Amigo entered into a contribution agreement with SchemeCo under which it would (i) make an initial payment of £15 million, to be held on trust in a '**Scheme Fund**', (ii) pay another sum up to £20 million into this Fund as valid claims were made and (iii) pay an amount equal to 15% of its annual consolidated profits before tax for the subsequent four years. Scheme Creditors were to submit claims within a six-month period, which SchemeCo would assess and value. Scheme Creditors would have the right to refer disputes to a **Scheme Adjudicator** (proposed to be the accounting firm Grant Thornton[66]). Claims not made within the six-month period would be barred. Agreed claims would be paid out from the Scheme Fund on a pro rata basis, in return for which Scheme Creditors' claims against Amigo would be released. **Scheme Supervisors** would be appointed to oversee the process and, under the scheme, would be authorised by the Scheme Creditors to execute a deed on their behalf releasing the company, PLC, certain other entities, and their directors and employees from all relevant claims. The expected recovery was 10 pence on the pound, although this was dependent on a number of variables and might be higher or lower.

3.4 The Role of the FCA

The Group had been in contact with the FCA, the UK's conduct regulator for financial services firms and markets, since November 2020 in relation to the scheme and had initially requested a 'letter of no-objection', as is the practice (although not a legal or regulatory requirement) in relation to financial firms. In discharge of its supervisory functions, the FCA assesses proposed schemes for compatibility with its rules of conduct, which are potentially broader than those employed by a court that might subsequently consider the scheme. In this case, after initial feedback, Amigo withdrew its request for a letter.[67]

66 [2021] EWHC 1002 (Ch), [7].
67 [2021] EWHC 1401 (Ch), [44].

3.5 *The First Convening Hearing*

At the convening hearing, the FCA was not represented but sent the court a letter stating that it did not support the proposed scheme. This was primarily for three reasons: (i) Redress Creditors would not receive the full value of their claims; (ii) the claims settlement process, which was partly automated, was less thorough than the methodology adopted by FOS; and (iii) the FCA did not welcome the six-month bar date. Ultimately, however, the FCA considered at the time of the convening hearing that these were all matters for the Scheme Creditors to take into account in deciding whether to vote for the scheme.[68] Trower J convened a single meeting for all Scheme Creditors.

3.6 *The First Scheme Creditors' Meeting*

Two days before the meeting, the FCA declared that, irrespective of the outcome, it would oppose the scheme being sanctioned.[69]

At the meeting in May 2021, 78,740 Scheme Creditors voted in person or by proxy. Of those voting, 95.1% in number, representing 95.7% of votes cast by value, voted in favour. This represented about 8.7% and 10% of the potential class by number and value, respectively, and included FOS.[70]

3.7 *The Sanction Hearing before Miles J*

At the sanction hearing, the FCA was represented by leading and junior counsel.[71] It raised several fundamental concerns about the structure and effect of the scheme and the information on the basis of which Scheme Creditors had been invited to cast their votes.

Firstly, the FCA noted that the shares in the Parent, which was to retain its economic stake in Amigo if the scheme were sanctioned, had increased in value by more than 250% since late December 2020, when the Group announced its intention to promote a scheme. The market capitalisation of the Group the day before the FCA announced its intention to oppose the scheme was about £140 million. Miles J accepted that this represented the market valuation of the equity in Amigo after taking account of Amigo's

68 [2021] EWHC 1002 (Ch), [12].
69 [2021] EWHC 1401 (Ch), [8].
70 [2021] EWHC 1401 (Ch), [64], [66].
71 By way of disclosure, seven of the 10 counsel who appeared before the Court in the four hearings in *Amigo* belong to the same Chambers as the present author.

proposed contributions under the scheme and that this represented the market's view that the scheme would shift value from unsecured creditors to shareholders.[72]

Second, the court rejected SchemeCo's contention that the only alternative to the proposed scheme was for Amigo as well as SchemeCo to enter insolvent administration.[73] The court had been provided with very limited information as to Amigo's ability to continue to trade in the event that the scheme was not sanctioned.[74] In particular, there were no cash flow projections to show that the Group would become insolvent.[75] Such evidence as had been made available did not bear out imminent insolvency. In particular, a 'financial summary' provided to the court showed that the Group's cash balance would not fall to zero until January 2024, when some of the Group's secured borrowing would come due,[76] and the FCA had engineered an informal moratorium on the payment of redress claims, which its counsel confirmed to the court it would be willing to continue in case sanction was refused and the Group's controllers were willing to explore another restructuring.[77] There was also the market's perception that "the Group has business – the brand, employees, infrastructure and so forth – to generate significant positive earnings in the future".[78] In the circumstances, the court agreed with the FCA that if the proposed scheme were not sanctioned, the Group and its controllers would have reasonable time to assess and promote further restructuring proposals.[79]

Third, the Group had not justified the proposed allocation of future value under the scheme. In particular, it had not explained why 15% of its future earnings over four years were to be channelled into the Scheme Fund, rather than a higher percentage of a longer period.[80] Further, while it was commonplace in restructurings for equity to take a hit, this was not the case under the proposed scheme.[81]

Fourth, Miles J considered that these issues would not necessarily be decisive to the scheme being sanctioned if the court could be satisfied that Scheme Creditors had been properly consulted and informed of their options and then had voted in favour of the scheme.[82] However, the information provided to Scheme Creditors had been deficient. The statutory Explan had not explained that the contributions into the Scheme Fund had been calculated by reference to the returns needed to be offered to investors for a

72 [2021] EWHC 1401 (Ch), [72]-[74].
73 [2021] EWHC 1401 (Ch), [96]-[97].
74 [2021] EWHC 1401 (Ch), [82].
75 [2021] EWHC 1401 (Ch), [84].
76 [2021] EWHC 1401 (Ch), [85].
77 [2021] EWHC 1401 (Ch), [86].
78 [2021] EWHC 1401 (Ch), [87].
79 [2021] EWHC 1401 (Ch), [83], [85], [87].
80 [2021] EWHC 1401 (Ch), [90].
81 [2021] EWHC 1401 (Ch), [78], [92].
82 [2021] EWHC 1401 (Ch), [77].

future rights issue. The information provided at the Scheme Creditors' meeting had been misleading in omitting to explain that PLC's equity was held not only by 8,000 retail investors who were not likely to be able to contribute further capital towards a restructuring but also by two institutional investors holding about 18% of equity who were.[83]

Fifth, the court accepted the FCA's contention that the proposed scheme was not fair. The English court usually proceeds on the basis that where a scheme (or plan) has been approved by the statutory majority, that majority is a better judge of its own interests than is the court. However, that presupposes that (i) the members of the class are capable of understanding what is proposed and (ii) of the alternatives open to them and that (iii) they have been provided with adequate information as to both these issues.[84] Here, the overwhelming majority of Scheme Creditors were financially vulnerable people who did not have access to mainstream credit and who had low levels of financial literacy, and who would likely have no understanding of corporate insolvency or restructurings.[85] Second, while in some previous cases involving such creditors the debtor company proposing a restructuring had paid for lawyers and financial advisors to advise creditors, this had not been done here.[86] Third, the scheme was not the outcome of negotiations between SchemeCo and Scheme Creditors but instead had been formulated unilaterally by the former and presented to the latter on a take-it-or-leave-it basis.[87] Fourth, the level of turnout at the meeting had been comparatively low.[88] Fifth, the Scheme Creditors had misleadingly been presented with a binary choice between the proposed scheme and insolvent administration[89] and had not been told the basis on which the shareholders were to retain all of the equity[90] or the reasons for the sharing of the value from the restructured business.[91]

Importantly, in refusing to sanction the scheme, Miles J appeared to give less weight to, or to have created an exception to, the principle, supported by '*ample authority*', that the court does not compare the actual scheme with hypothetical alternatives.[92] He stated that that principle is premised on proper consultation with creditors based on the provision of full and fair information about the scheme.[93] The Judge ended by "*urg[ing] the directors to continue their efforts to promote a suitable restructuring*".[94]

83 [2021] EWHC 1401 (Ch), [71], [91].
84 [2021] EWHC 1401 (Ch), [100]-[102].
85 [2021] EWHC 1401 (Ch), [105].
86 [2021] EWHC 1401 (Ch), [106].
87 [2021] EWHC 1401 (Ch), [108]-[112].
88 [2021] EWHC 1401 (Ch), [113]-[117].
89 [2021] EWHC 1401 (Ch), [132]-[133].
90 [2021] EWHC 1401 (Ch), [134].
91 [2021] EWHC 1401 (Ch), [135].
92 [2021] EWHC 1401 (Ch), [140].
93 [2021] EWHC 1401 (Ch), [141].
94 [2021] EWHC 1401 (Ch), [143].

3.8 *The Revised Proposal and Its Sanction*

Miles J proved "*prescient*".[95] Contrary to their protestations, neither Amigo nor the Group entered insolvent administration upon the court's refusal to sanction the scheme. Instead, SchemeCo came back to court in March 2022 (i.e. a year later) with not one but two new schemes proposed in the alternative, one (the New Business Scheme or '**NBS**') premised on the FCA permitting Amigo to start lending again and the other (the Wind-Down Scheme or '**WDS**') on Amigo being unable to resume lending. Both diluted existing shareholders to 5%, with the NBS and WDS offering 41p and 33p on the pound to Scheme Creditors, respectively, with a projected 31p likely to go to them in administration.[96] A solicitor was appointed at the Group's expense as '*Customer Advocate*' and "*with a wide remit to liaise with customers and other interested bodies, to review the materials provided by Amigo and to provide a report to the Court on any issues arising relevant to the convening hearing*".[97] There was still, however, a six-month bar date and the same claims management process.[98] The schemes were approved. FCA withdrew its opposition and did not appear at the sanction hearing, in May 2022,[99] at which Trower J sanctioned the scheme.

3.9 *Reflections*

The *Amigo* saga can be regarded as an instance of English restructuring practice working efficaciously to weed out an opportunistic lowball proposal pitched at a creditor class consisting of vulnerable retail creditors of whom a vast majority of those choosing to vote had approved the proposal and forcing the debtor's management to come up with a fairer restructuring while preserving the undoubtedly insolvent debtor's going concern.

In my view, two factors proved key to this outcome.

First, and as should be obvious from the foregoing account, the involvement of the FCA was decisive. Acting as the primary debtor's supervisor and in discharge of its statutory duty to protect users of financial services, the FCA was able to intervene effectively, through highly experienced restructuring counsel, forensically to pinpoint the many deficiencies in both substance and process. This carried very significant weight with the court.

Second, and possibly less obvious, was the influence of the four Judges who presided over the four hearings. English counsel sometimes distinguish between '*merits judges*',

95 As Snowden LJ observed drily a year later: [2022] EWHC 549 (Ch), [18].
96 [2022] EWHC 549 (Ch), [40].
97 [2022] EWHC 549 (Ch), [46].
98 [2022] EWHC 549 (Ch), [27]-[28].
99 [2022] EWHC 1318 (Ch), [10].

who focus primarily on whether they approve of the proposed outcome on fairness or utilitarian grounds and then consider whether there are insurmountable legal objections to achieving that outcome, and '*technical judges*', who focus firstly on whether what is proposed can be achieved in law and give less weight to their sense of the merits. This distinction is crude, can be misleading, and is untenable if pushed even a little too far. All judges are likely to give some weight to both sets of considerations and probably to give differing weight to them from case to case. Further, on the facts, as the preceding account should show, there were both 'technical' and 'merits' problems with the original scheme.

My picture of *Amigo* would, nevertheless, be left partly unpainted if I were not to note that the first convening hearing in March 2021 was presided over by Sir Alastair Norris, who, while in my respectful view an excellent technical lawyer, may fairly be characterised, overall, as a merits judge, and who (noting again the FCA's absence from that hearing) did not give any indication that he considered there to be a '*blot*' on the proposed scheme.

Miles J, who presided over the key sanction hearing in May 2021, was not a restructuring specialist and had not conducted a restructuring hearing before. In addition to have mastered the long-established principles governing restructuring, he can be regarded as having brought a fresh perspective to them, as indicated by his discounting the principle that the court does not compare an actual scheme or plan with hypothetical alternatives. His judgment is, in my view, an exemplar of judgecraft, combining technical virtuosity, regard for principle, creativity and practical wisdom in just about the right proportions.

Snowden LJ, who presided over the second convening meeting in March 2022, was one of the leading restructuring counsel before rising to the Bench and is amongst the judges before whom restructuring counsel aware of weaknesses in their case most fear appearing. While ever mindful of merits to which, in my view, he invariably gives due weight, Snowden LJ is a technical judge par excellence. He described Miles J's judgment as "*comprehensive and penetrating*",[100] and notwithstanding the withdrawal of opposition from the FCA, took a noticeably more searching attitude towards the second scheme.

The final sanction hearing in May 2022 was presided over by Trower J, another leading restructuring counsel[101] before going to the Bench, who it would again be fair to characterise, overall, as a merits judge. In the circumstances, any observer of the London restructuring market would have been able to predict ex ante that the scheme would be sanctioned.

100 [2022] EWCH 549 (Ch), [15].
101 And, by way of disclosure, this author's former Head of Chambers.

The point, put simply, is that the identity of the presiding judge matters and that it may matter decisively. This is perhaps inevitable in a discretion-heavy system such as that in England, with attendant benefits and costs.

4. Conclusion

I conclude by comparing the current state of English law with the recommendations for the improvement of the US system made by Lindsey Simon.[102] The overarching point of difference is between the rule-based obligation approach favoured by Simon and the discretionary, show-it-or-be-presumed-to-lack-it approach of English restructuring law.

Firstly, Simon recommends that the real debtors (whose liabilities are to be discharged) be required to make the same disclosures as are mandated for the (nominal) debtors who have proposed the restructuring, including as to their assets and liabilities, financial statements and monthly operating reports.[103] In England, the restructuring process effectively operates as a 'pre-pack', with the formal, court-based phase not lasting more than a couple of months. Therefore, monthly operating reports are less relevant. However, the nominal debtor is required to provide adequate information in a form appropriate to the nature of creditors, and, as *Amigo* shows, this information must, in practice, extend to the real and not merely the nominal debtor. If it does not, the court may withhold sanction.

Second, Simon favours the extension of the *'341 meeting*', a form of bankruptcy deposition, to real debtors.[104] There is nothing comparable in English law, though, in practice, debtors often organise pre-meeting Q&A sessions or similar with proposed creditors. The utility of such sessions is likely to vary from case to case.

Third, Simon recommends standard civil law procedural practices being extended to creditors, including an opt-out process for individual members of the creditor class, the opportunity to provide supporting evidence to receive an individualised prorated amount rather than a flat one, an automatic right of appeal, an independent arbiter and meaningful payment of awarded claims.[105] As shown by the *Amigo* case study, it is up to the company (or other applicant) proposing the restructuring in England to decide whether any of these mechanisms is included in the proposal. However, again, the absence of any of these mechanisms may, depending on the facts, count, perhaps heavily, against sanction.

Fourth, Simon favours extension of a variant of the '*best interest test*' to the creditors of the real debtor. This should enable creditors to assess and compare where they

---

102 In Lindsey Simon, 'Bankruptcy Grifters' (2022) 131 *Yale LJ* 1154, 1205 *et seq*.
103 Simon, 'Grifters', 1207-1209.
104 Simon, 'Grifters', 1209-1210.
105 Simon, 'Grifters', 1210-1211.

stand if the restructuring is and is not approved.[106] The *Amigo* cases show the very significant importance of this factor in English restructuring practice.

Fifth, Simon considers that the restructuring should only be approved if funded by the securities and a majority of voting shares in one or more real debtors.[107] Again, while this is not a legal requirement, *Amigo* shows that the absence of equity holders' sacrifice may count heavily against sanction.

106 Simon, 'Grifters,' 1212-1214.
107 Simon, 'Grifters,' 1214-1215.

Third-Party Releases under Dutch Law since the WHOA: A Warm Welcome for a Very Limited Number of Guests Only?

Sid Pepels[*]

1. Introduction

Although third-party releases in creditor schemes[1] have been a familiar sight under US and UK law for quite some time now, their occurrence under Dutch law has thus far been fairly limited. Prior to the enactment of the *Wet Homologatie Onderhands Akkoord* (the **WHOA**) on 1 January 2021, Dutch law only provided for court confirmation of creditor schemes in court supervised formal insolvency proceedings: the Dutch suspension of payments (*surseance van betaling*) and bankruptcy (*faillissement*) proceedings. Although there are examples where creditor schemes were successfully used to restructure companies' debts in either of the two formal proceedings,[2] they were rather rare in Dutch insolvency law. If this report had been written ten years ago, a couple of pages would have likely sufficed.[3]

With the introduction of the Dutch preventive scheme proceedings outside of formal insolvency under the WHOA (hereinafter also referred to as the **Dutch Preventive Scheme**), the discussion on third-party releases under Dutch law has also entered a new stage. The WHOA has significantly increased the (potential for) Dutch creditor schemes in relation to companies in distress. Debtors, creditors, insolvency professionals and judges alike will likely see themselves increasingly confronted with questions

---

* Attorney-at-law at Jones Day Amsterdam; external PhD candidate at the Radboud University with a focus on cross-border restructurings of groups of companies under the EU Insolvency Regulation (recast).

1 The term 'creditor schemes' is used throughout this report as a reference to (*schuldeisers*)*akkoorden* both in- and outside of insolvency proceedings, depending on the context, also commonly referred to as 'composition plans', 'creditor compositions' or 'restructuring plans'.

2 Creditor schemes in suspension of payment proceedings have proven particularly helpful to restructure bond (*obligatie*) debt; *see, e.g.*, the restructurings of Global Telecom Systems (GTS), Versatel, UPC, Plaza Centers and the Oi Group.

3 *See, e.g.*, the 2011 dissertation of Anna Soedira on the creditor scheme under Dutch law, which required three pages to deal with this topic. Anna Soedira, Het Akkoord (Dissertation, Radboud University Nijmegen, 2011) 93-96.

concerning the admissibility and appropriateness of third-party releases in creditor schemes.

This report (*preadvies*) aims to analyse the extent to which Dutch law allows the imposition of third-party releases included in creditor schemes on creditors. In doing so, the report starts by providing some background to the discussion in Section 2 and continues with a brief historical *tour d'horizon* of the legal landscape prior to the enactment of the WHOA in Section 3. Section 4 discusses the options to apply third-party releases in Dutch Preventive Schemes and concludes with a discussion on the (potential for) application of third-party releases outside the scope of the WHOA provisions in Section 5.

2. What Are Third-Party Releases and Why Are They Relevant?

But before diving into Dutch law, it is worthwhile to briefly discuss what should be understood by 'third-party releases' and what their relevance is in relation to creditor schemes.

Generally, only a single legal entity is the subject of (pre-)insolvency proceedings.[4] Creditor schemes prepared in such proceedings typically deal with the capital structure of that particular debtor, for example by allowing a (partial) write-down of its debt, possibly in exchange for an equity stake in the debtor. As a starting point, creditor schemes generally do not affect the liabilities that third parties may have incurred in connection with the relevant debtor.[5] However, for differing categories of liabilities and for differing reasons, the release of claims against third parties (also referred to as non-debtor parties) may be conducive or even necessary for the successful implementation of a creditor scheme.[6]

---

4 *See, e.g.*, CJEU 2 May 2006, C-341/04 (*Eurofood IFSC Ltd.*), para. 30; CJEU 15 December 2011, C-191/10 (*Rastelli*), paras. 13-29. *See* on the single entity approach, *e.g.*, Sid Pepels 'Cross-border CoCo in group insolvencies under the Recast EIR and the existence of an 'overriding group interest' – One for all, and all for one?' (2021) 5 EIRJ, para. 2.

5 Michael Veder and Adrian Thery, 'The release of third party guarantees in pre-insolvency restructuring plans', in Faber and others (eds), Trust and Good Faith Across Borders (Liber Amicorum Prof. dr. S.C.J.J. Kortmann) (Wolters Kluwer 2017) 265-266. *See also* Ilya Kokorin, 'Third Part Releases in Insolvency of Multinational Enterprise Grounds' (2021) 18 ECFR 107, note 34.

6 *Cf.* Christian Pilkington, Schemes of Arrangement in Corporate Restructuring (2 edn, Sweet & Maxwell 2020) para. 9-001 *ff.*

2.1 *Category 1: Corporate Guarantees*

Third-party releases will often be useful in relation to debt that already existed prior to the restructuring. The application of third-party releases within the context of groups of companies is a prime example thereof.[7] Group companies are often financially intertwined, for instance as a result of group financing facilities and pursuant to, in particular, guarantees, sureties, joint and several liabilities and cross-collateralization (e.g. *garanties, borgtocht, hoofdelijkheid* or *derdenzekerheid*, hereinafter, for ease of reference, all referred to as guarantees). The financial distress of one group company will often topple other companies within the group as well as a result of these entanglements.[8] Where, for instance, a distressed group company is only able to pay 60 per cent of the guaranteed claims against a release thereof, the remaining 40 per cent will have to come out of the other group companies' pockets. If those group companies have insufficient funds available to (immediately) repay those remaining amounts, they may end up in restructuring or liquidation proceedings themselves as well, constituting a domino effect.[9]

This effect is further magnified by the group companies' interdependency. While groups of companies comprise legally separate group members, they will often economically, financially, administratively and/or operationally function as integrated and interdependent businesses.[10] If one group company is restructured but other companies pertaining to the same group subsequently fail because they cannot pay their guaranteed obligations, that subsequent financial distress within the group will often again impact the restructured group company because of this interdependency, or even because event-of-default or acceleration clauses in group financing facilities may be retriggered.

Third-party release clauses allow the restructuring of certain cross-indebtedness among group companies, without having to open individual proceedings for all group companies involved with all the value destructive effects that such proceedings may have. This could, for instance, involve the restructuring only of not a company's liabil-

---

7 *See, e.g.*, on this topic Veder and Thery (n 5) 259; Anne Mennens, Het Dwangakkoord buiten Surseance en Faillissement (Wolters Kluwer 2020) 495, 507-508; Kokorin (n 5); Sid Pepels, 'De WHOA als instrument voor (grensoverschrijdende) groepsherstructureringen' (2021) 1 MvO 1, para. 4.

8 *See* for an extensive analysis on the specific problems relating to (cross-border) group insolvency proceedings: Irit Mevorach, Insolvency Within Multinational Enterprise Groups (Oxford University Press 2009), more in particular Chapter 2: *"To Link or not to Link?" The Problem of the Multinational Enterprise Group Business Structure*.

9 *Cf.* Klaus Siemon and Frank Frind, 'Groups of Companies in Insolvency: A German Perspective: Overcoming the Domino Effect in an (International) Group Insolvency' (2013) 22(2) IIR 61, 68; Pepels (n 4) 5.

10 *E.g.* because the group's back office functions or financial management is centralized (*e.g.* via cash pooling), because business units comprise employees of multiple group companies (which may, *e.g.*, be the case in groups where companies are separated along geographical lines) or because one group company depends on products or services provided by another group company in order to produce or service itself. *See* further on forms of integration within groups of companies: Mevorach (n 8) para. 5.3.2.

ity but also of claims pursuant to guarantees provided by a parent company for (certain) debt of the subsidiary, as is demonstrated in Figure 1:

Figure 1. (Overview Third Parties – Guarantees)

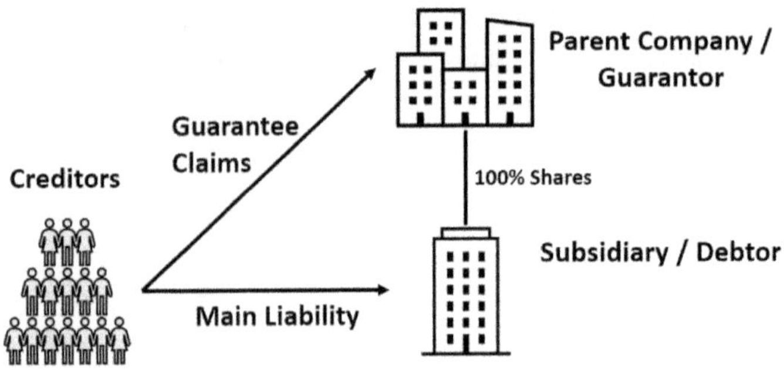

Guarantees may also be provided by other legal entities than group companies, e.g. by the natural person who owns the relevant debtor company (and who, as such, may also be its director).

2.2 *Category 2: Third Parties Liable under Tort Pre-Restructuring*

The second category of pre-existing debt concerns the involvement of (*de facto*) directors, shareholders and other parties with the company (or their respective insurers) prior to the opening of the (pre) insolvency proceedings. They may see a creditor scheme as an opportunity for a release of their own liability against the company's creditors relating to (potentially) tortious acts prior to the restructuring.[11] This may incentivize (*de facto*) directors, shareholders or their insurers to (substantially) contribute to the insolvency estate to enable a creditor scheme in exchange for their release:

11 *E.g.* as a result of (de facto) directors' or shareholders' liability or in relation to transaction avoidance claims or guarantees.

Figure 2. (Overview Third Parties – Pre-restructuring)

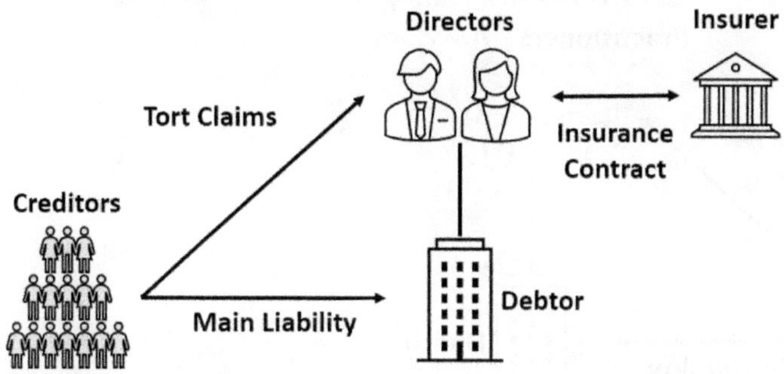

The creditor scheme may then even effectively be applied as an alternative mechanism to deal with mass harm (*massaschade*).[12] The American Chapter 11 bankruptcy proceeding of *Purdue Pharma LP*, discussed by co-reporters Simon and Brubaker in their reports, is a controversial example of this application of third-party releases.

Vriesendorp and Hermans argued during the legislative process concerning the WHOA that the application of creditor schemes in this manner may function as a driver for value maximization for the relevant creditors without the need for complex and costly litigation.[13]

2.3 *Category 3: Decision Makers and Advisors Involved with the Restructuring or Insolvency*

A third category of liability concerning which third-party release clauses may be useful concerns key decision-makers and advisors that partake in the relevant restructurings or insolvency proceedings, such as the debtor's directors, lawyers, financial advisors, insolvency practitioners and their firms and/or employees:

12 Since the enactment of the *Wet collectieve afwikkeling massaschade* (WCAM) in 2005, replaced per 1 January 2020 by the *Wet Afwikkeling Massaschade in Collectieve Actie* (WAMCA), Dutch law provides for a general systematic approach to collectively deal with such mass harm claims outside the scope of restructuring or insolvency proceedings.

13 Ruud Hermans and Reinout Vriesendorp, 'Het dwangakkoord in het insolventierecht: vrijheid in gebondenheid?' (2014) 10 TvI 94, para. 4.

Figure 3. (Overview Third Parties – Decision-Makers)

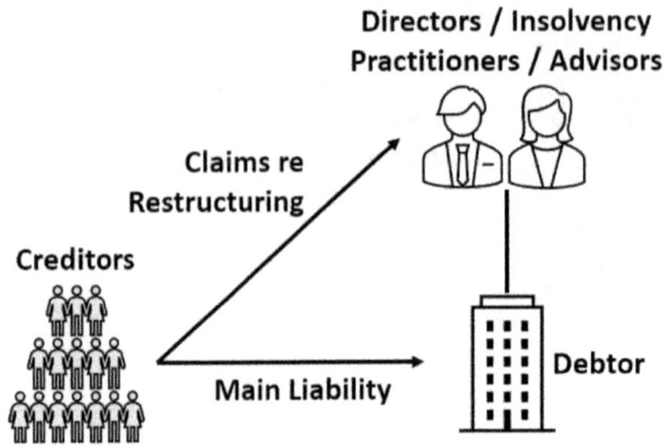

Corporate financial restructurings and insolvencies often deal with large sums of money. The key decision makers and advisors involved therein thus expose themselves to substantial risks. Any decision that plays out wrongly, no matter how small, may result in insurmountable damages claims. The release of claims that creditors of the debtor may have against those decision makers involved in the negotiation, formalization and implementation of a creditor scheme and their advisors may, for instance, give them sufficient comfort to make key decisions for the restructuring.

It has been argued that key decision makers and their advisors may be reluctant to expose themselves to certain risks, absent such a release.[14] For the same reason, releases of such parties may also significantly lower the fees against which they are willing and able to contribute to the restructuring or insolvency.[15]

3. Third-Party Releases in the Netherlands Prior to the Dutch Preventive Scheme – Theory and Practice

3.1 The Legal Framework: A Conservative Approach

As will be further discussed later, the WHOA explicitly provides for the release of third-party liability, although the relevant statutory provision only deals with group guarantees and only allows a release under certain conditions. This report will further deal with

14 Pilkington (n 6) para. 9-002-9-006. *Cf.* also Mennens (n 4) 503-504. *See*, in particular, her reference to the Lehman Brothers International (Europe) Scheme.

15 *Ibid.*

the question of what those conditions are and to what extent third-party release clauses are admissible in relation to Categories 2 and 3 and for group guarantees outside the WHOA. But before doing so, the following will first provide some necessary historical background to the legal landscape prior to the enactment of the WHOA.

Starting in the mid-nineties and spearheaded by Soedira[16] and Kortmann,[17] the majority of Dutch authors who have contributed on this topic have assumed that third-party releases in creditor schemes could only be invoked against creditors who voted in favour of that scheme but not against non-consenting creditors (which term refers to both rejecting and non-voting creditors).[18] Such 'extraneous scheme provisions' or '*akkoordvreemde bepalingen*' should not affect creditors' positions vis-à-vis non-debtor third parties without their explicit consent. These scholars generally base their position on the creditor scheme's nature as an agreement between the debtor and its creditors and thus only concerning the creditor-debtor relationship and the distribution of the debtor's estate.[19] Third-party release clauses would be a supplement to the creditor scheme, not a part of it.[20] As such, the binding effect of the court's confirmation decision would not extend to third-party release clauses. Creditors who voted in favour of the creditor scheme would not be bound to a third-party release clause included therein by virtue of the scheme's confirmation by the court but, rather, under general Dutch contract law as a result of their consent (*aanvaarding*).[21] Assuming the third-party releases would be drafted as a third-party stipulation (*derdenbeding*), the non-debtor party could invoke that third-party release from the moment it has accepted that stipulation.[22]

16 Anna Soedira 'De inhoud van een akkoord', in: Bas Kortmann and Dennis Faber (eds), De curator, een octopus (W.E.J. Tjeenk Willink 1996) 219, 223 ff.

17 Bas Kortmann, 'Derden in het faillissementsrecht' (1997) 46 AA 5, 59-60.

18 *See, e.g.*, Soedira (n 16); Soedira (n 3); Kortmann (n 17); Karen Harmsen, 'Lehman Brothers: een akkoord in strijd met de Faillissementswet' (2013) 28 TvI; W.J.M. van Andel in *JOR* 2013/191 with Amsterdam District Court 22 March 2013, ECLI:NL:RBAMS:2013:BZ5246; Dennis Faber, Frédéric Verhoeven and Niels Vermunt, 'The use of a composition plan as a valuation and distribution framework' in: Dennis Faber and Niels Vermunt (eds), Bank Failure: Lessons from Lehman Brothers (Oxford University Press 2017) para. 12.91-93; Mennens (n 14) 495 *ff*; Bob Wessels, Het Akkoord (Wessels Insolventierecht nr. VI) (5 edn, Wolters Kluwer 2020) para. 6159 *ff*. *See also* questioning the validity of third-party release clauses included in the Lehman Brothers Treasury Co B.V. creditor scheme: Opinion of the Advocate-General Timmerman dated 13 February 2013, *JOR* 2013/190 (Lehman Brothers Finance/Lehman Brothers Treasury cs), part 2.47. *See* more lenient towards allowing third-party releases: Christiaan Zijderveld and Ida Nylund, 'Reactie op 'Lehman Brothers: een akkoord in strijd met de Faillissementswet'' (2013) 28 TvI; Hermans and Vriesendorp (n 13) 49; Nicolaes Tollenaar, Het pre-insolventieakkoord, Grondslagen en raamwerk (Wolters Kluwer 2016) 300-302.

19 *See* Soedira (n 16) 225-226; Soedira (n 3); Kortmann (n 17); Faber, Verhoeven and Vermunt (n 18) par. 12.92; Mennens (n 14) 498-499.

20 *See* Soedira (n 16) 224; Soedira (n 3) 94-95.

21 *See* Kortmann (n 17) 321-322; Soedira (n 16) 93-96; Faber, Verhoeven and Vermunt (n 18) para 12.92; Mennens (n 14) 497, in particular, note 278.

22 *See* Art. 6:254(1) Dutch Civil Code. *See* Kortmann (n 17) 60; Soedira (n 16) 96; Faber, Verhoeven and Vermunt 2017 (n 18) para. 12.93.

In addition to the creditor schemes' nature (the rationale behind) Article 160 of the Dutch Bankruptcy Act (*de Faillissementswet*, hereinafter also referred to as the **DBA**) is often referenced.[23] This provision prescribes that a creditor scheme offered in a bankruptcy proceeding does not affect the rights of creditors against providers of guarantees and co-debtors of the scheme debtor:

> "Regardless of the creditor scheme, the creditors maintain all their rights against surety providers and other co-debtors of the debtor. The rights that they can exercise on assets of third parties are maintained as if no creditor scheme came about."[24]

With the implementation of the provisions on creditor schemes in suspension of payments proceedings (*surseance van betaling*) in 1935, Article 160 DBA was declared applicable to schemes in suspension of payments proceedings.[25]

Further support for this position is found in the 1990 Dutch Supreme Court judgment in the *De Maes Janssens* case.[26] In this judgment the Dutch Supreme Court ruled, referencing Article 160 DBA and the rationale behind it, that a creditor who had received payment of a percentage of its claim pursuant to a creditor scheme against release of its remaining claim on the debtor was not prohibited from claiming the remaining percentages of its claim on a third party on the basis of a tort claim (*onrechtmatige daadsvorderingen*):

> "The Bankruptcy Act considers the creditor scheme to be an agreement and there is no ground to have this agreement benefit a third party from whom the creditor has recourse concerning the non-payment of his claim on the debtor on account of a wrongful act committed against him by the third party. The latter would also not be in accordance with the system of the Bankruptcy Act and in particular with the provisions of article 160 DBA according to which a creditor, despite the fact that he receives percentages on his claim pursuant to the scheme, nevertheless retains all his rights against the guarantors and on

---

23 *See, e.g.*, Soedira (n 16) 225-226; Kortmann (n 17) 322; Faber, Verhoeven and Vermunt (n 18) para. 12.92; Mennens (n 14) 498-499. Note that Soedira and Mennens both state that the impossibility of imposing third-party releases on non-consenting creditors could be concluded without necessarily relying on Art. 160 DBA, but already follows from the nature of a Dutch creditor scheme. Kortmann also refers to Art. 160 DBA as an "additional argument".

24 Informal translation. In Dutch "Niettegenstaande het akkoord behouden de schuldeisers al hun rechten tegen de borgen en andere medeschuldenaren van de schuldenaar. De rechten, welke zij op goederen van derden kunnen uitoefenen, blijven bestaan als ware geen akkoord tot stand gekomen."

25 *See* Art. 272(6) DBA, previously Section 5. *See* similarly on the provisions for debt relief for natural persons (*Wet schuldsanering natuurlijke personen*), Art. 340(4) DBA.

26 *See, e.g.*, Kortmann (n 17) 59-60; Soedira (n 16); Soedira (n 3) 95; Mennens (n 14) 498.

> the goods connected to him by third parties: accordingly, it must be assumed that the creditor also retains his right of recourse against the aforementioned third party."[27]

In other words, the Dutch Supreme Court also ruled out the (automatic) release of third-party liabilities in cases that are not directly covered by Article 160 DBA (i.e. tort claims instead of guarantees). The ruling is clear: creditor schemes are not intended to benefit third parties on whom a creditor may recover the unpaid portion of its claim.

The Attorney-General Hartkamp was equally clear in its wording:

> "The matter at hand concerns no joint and several liability or a related legal concept [...]: the claim of the [creditor] against [the bankrupt person] has an entirely different basis than the – alleged – claim against [the third party] (credit agreement vs. wrongful act). The solution chosen in article 160 DBA must apply in this case a fortiori. It is hard to see how the creditor scheme can lead to the extinction of a right in tort against a third party (a capacity which, in this case, [the third party] can also be regarded)."[28]

3.2 *Practice: Third-Party Release Clauses Used but Untested*

Although the majority of legal scholars generally assumed that third-party release clauses would only work in relation to consenting creditors, Dutch creditor schemes have, in practice, often included third-party release clauses in some form or another. The creditor scheme for the *Stichting Wereldruiterspelen 1994* is an oft-cited example.[29] The

27 Dutch Supreme Court, 18 May 1990, *NJ* 1991, 412, m. nt. MMM, para 3.2. Informal translation. In Dutch: "De Faillissementswet beschouwt het akkoord als een overeenkomst en er is geen grond deze overeenkomst ten voordele te doen strekken van een derde op wie de schuldeiser verhaal heeft ter zake van het niet voldaan zijn van zijn vordering op de schuldenaar uit hoofde van een door de derde jegens hem gepleegde onrechtmatige daad. Dit laatste zou ook niet stroken met het stelsel van de Faillissementswet en met name niet met het bepaalde in artikel 160 Fw volgens hetwelk een schuldeiser, ondanks het feit dat hij de akkoordpercenten over zijn vordering ontvangt, niettemin al zijn rechten tegen de borgen en op het hem door derden verbonden goed behoudt: dienovereenkomstig moet worden aangenomen dat de schuldeiser ook zijn verhaalsrecht op evenbedoelde derde behoudt."

28 Opinion A-G Hartkamp to the Dutch Supreme Court's 18 May 1990 judgment (*NJ* 1991, 412), par. 2. Informal translation. In Dutch: "In het onderhavige geval is van hoofdelijkheid of een daarmee verwante rechtsfiguur [...] geen sprake: de vordering van de [schuldeiser] jegens [de failliet] heeft een geheel andere grondslag dan de – gepretendeerde – vordering jegens [de derde] (kredietovereenkomst resp. onrechtmatige daad). Hier moet de in artikel 160 Fw gekozen oplossing a fortiori gelden. Niet valt in te zien hoe het faillissementsakkoord kan leiden tot het tenietgaan van een recht uit onrechtmatige daad jegens een derde (als hoedanigheid i.c. ook [de derde] is te beschouwen)."

29 Utrecht District Court 6 April 1994, 02.02.671/94. Although unpublished, it is discussed in Soedira (n 16) 233; Soedira (n 3) 93 *ff*; Kortmann (n 17) 60; Mennens (n 14) 496.

scheme stipulated that by voting in favour of it, the creditors would irrevocably waive their 'presumed claims' ('*vermeende vorderingsrechten*') against the Stichting's directors and their insurers.[30] It is not entirely clear whether the scheme is intended to only waive the consenting creditors' claims against the directors and their insurers or whether a general waiver was assumed.[31] In any event, the scheme was confirmed by the Utrecht District Court.[32]

The creditor scheme in the Dutch bankruptcy of Lehman Brothers Treasury Co. B.V. (**LBT**) included a third-party release for, among others, LBT, its current and future directors and bankruptcy trustees (*curatoren*) in relation to – in short – liability resulting from the Dutch insolvency proceedings and the execution of the creditor scheme offered therein.[33] While criticized in the literature, partially in relation to the included third-party releases,[34] the LBT creditor scheme was confirmed by the Amsterdam District Court and not further effectively challenged.[35]

Similarly, the creditor schemes in the bankruptcy proceedings concerning Plaza Centers N.V., the two Dutch entities involved in the Brazilian Oi Group insolvency (Oi Brasil Holdings Coöperatief U.A.[36] and Portugal Telecom International Finance B.V.) and the Intertoys Group insolvency[37] all included broad third-party releases, for instance relating to all claims against relevant group companies; the current, former and future directors; direct and indirect shareholders; and the bankruptcy trustees and

30 Soedira (n 3) 93, quoting Clause 3 of the respective creditor scheme: "Door voor het ontwerp van akkoord te stemmen doen de schuldeisers, doch uitsluitend voor het geval dat het akkoord wordt aanvaard en gehomologeerd, onherroepelijk afstand van hun vermeende vorderingsrechten op de bestuurders van de Stichting en hun verzekeraars, uit welke hoofde dan ook." Informally translated into "By voting in favour of the draft creditor scheme, the creditors, but only in the event that the agreement is accepted and confirmed, irrevocably waive their alleged rights of action against the directors of the Foundation and their insurers, on any grounds whatsoever".

31 Soedira (n 3) 94.

32 Soedira (n 16) 223 and in particular note 27.

33 *See* 'Composition Plan Lehman Brothers Treasury Co B.V.' of 5 December 2012, Art. 8 and the definition for 'Released Parties' at p. 26. The LBT Composition Plan is available via www.lehmanbrotherstreasury.com. All links to webpages in this Report were last verified on 8 June 2022.

34 *See, e.g.*, Harmsen (n 18), who argued, in line with Soedira and Kortmann, that a third-party release would not be able to bind non-consenting third parties. In the further back-and-forth that ensued between Harmsen and Zijderveld & Nylund (*see* TvI 2013/44 and 45), the validity of the third-party releases in the LBT creditor scheme remained undiscussed. *See also* the contribution of Faber, Verhoeven and Vermunt (18), who concluded, in para. 12.93, that only "eligible voting parties who have voted in favour of the adoption of the LBT composition plan are – in line with the prevailing opinion in legal literature and practice – bound to the third-party release clause contained in the LBT composition plan". Verhoeven was one of LBT's bankruptcy trustees.

35 *See* Harmsen (n 18).

36 I was involved in the insolvency proceedings concerning Oi Brasil Holdings Coöperatief U.A. as lawyer to the bankruptcy trustee.

37 Intertoys Holding B.V., Intertoys Holland B.V., Speelhoorn B.V. and Speelgoedpaleis Bart Smit B.V. I was involved in this bankruptcy proceeding as part of the insolvency trustees' team.

their firms. Each set of third-party releases was, however, limited "*to the extent permitted by law*".[38] The extent of this qualification has remained untested in court.

The creditor scheme that was confirmed in the suspension of payments proceedings concerning Steinhoff International Holdings N.V. in 2021 similarly included, among other things, certain third-party release clauses that released directors, group companies, their insurers and advisors from their potential liability vis-à-vis the creditors that were part of the Scheme.[39]

While the Dutch academy thus appears mostly united in its stance that third-party release in Dutch creditor schemes are not effective against non-consenting creditors, in practice it is not uncommon for such clauses to end up in schemes in some form or another, without their limits being tested.

4. The Dutch Preventive Scheme Enters the Stage: A Mechanism for Group Guarantee Releases

In response to the historically high number of bankruptcy proceedings that followed the 2007/2008 financial crisis and the subsequent economic crises, the Dutch legislature decided in 2012 to update the DBA and, among other things, include a statutory procedure for creditor schemes outside of suspension of payments or bankruptcy proceedings.[40] The discussion concerning third-party releases entered a new stage then, as the Dutch legislature, academy and practice were presented with a blank canvas to sketch a new form of proceeding. Several authors, including Vriesendorp, Hermans and De

38 *See, e.g.*, Art. 3.5.15 of the Plaza Centers creditor scheme "Each Plan Creditor hereby releases, to the extent permitted by law, the Company and all other companies of the Group, the current and former directors and officers of the Group, all direct and indirect shareholders of the Group (and their respective directors, officers, employees, agents, counsels or anyone acting on their behalf), from any and all liability under any applicable law other than with respect to claims or demands regarding which the grounds are fraud or malice or other ground for which a release is not permitted by law." The plan is available via http://plazacenters.com/index.php?p=debt_restructuring. *See* para. 65 of the Oi Coop creditor scheme, in conjunction with the definition for 'Released Parties' on p. 20 and for PTIF *see* para. 3.5 and the definition for 'Released Parties' on p. 6. *See* Art. 3.5.2 of the respective Intertoys creditor schemes and the definition for 'Released Parties' in Art. 1.2. The Intertoys Schemes did not include a waiver of claims concerning group companies.

39 *See* 'Steinhoff International Holdings N.V. Composition Plan' (8 September 2021) www.steinhoffinternational.com/settlement-litigation-claims.php.

40 *Kamerstukken II* 2010/11,29911 nr. 74, para. 2.

Vries,[41] as well as Tollenaar,[42] argued in favour of some form of third-party releases to be included in what ended up becoming the WHOA.

Inspired by the works of Hermans and Vriesendorp and referencing the benefits of third-party releases in the context of groups of companies,[43] the Dutch legislature opted to include a statutory mechanism for third-party releases explicitly related to claims of the principal debtor's creditors on companies that pertain to the same group as the debtor. Article 372(1) DBA, which entered into force on 1 January 2021, now reads:

> "A scheme as referred to in article 370(1) may also provide for the amendment of creditors' rights in respect of legal entities which form a group with the debtor as referred to in article 24b of Book 2 of the Dutch Civil Code...."[44]

In addition to the released non-debtor party pertaining to the same group of companies, the application of this provision requires that[45]

(a) the rights of the relevant creditors against that group company serve to pay or secure the payment of any obligations of the principal debtor, or of any obligations for which the group company is liable with or in addition to the principal debtor (which needs to be attributed broad meaning, e.g., also including abstract guarantees and group financing where not the group company offering the creditor scheme but the non-debtor group company is actually the main debtor under that financing);

(b) the group company – like the main debtor – is in a situation in which it may reasonably be expected that it will not be able to continue paying its debts;

---

41 *See* draft Art. 381 DBA in the legislative proposal on a Dutch extrajudicial creditors' scheme of Vriesendorp, Hermans and De Vries: Reinout Vriesendorp, Ruud Hermans and Klaas de Vries, 'Wetsvoorstel tot aanpassing van de Faillissementswet door uitbreiding met titel IV', 20 (2013) TvI 1. *See also* Hermans and Vriesendorp (n 13) para. 4.

42 Tollenaar (n 18) 300-302.

43 *See* re the first legislative proposal for the *Wet continuïteit ondernemingen II*, the WHOA's predecessor: Explanatory Note (*Memorie van Toelichting*) 'Wijziging van de Faillissementswet in verband met de invoering van de mogelijkheid tot het algemeen verbindend verklaren van een buiten faillissement gesloten akkoord ter herstructurering van de schulden (Wet continuïteit ondernemingen II)', consultatievoorstel 14 augustus 2014, pp. 48-49. The legislator also references the European Commission's recommendations, including the recommendation to limit the costs of a reorganisation as much as possible. Available via www.internetconsultatie.nl/wco2/details.

44 Informal translation. In Dutch: "Een akkoord als bedoeld in artikel 370, eerste lid, kan ook voorzien in de wijziging van rechten van schuldeisers jegens rechtspersonen die samen met de schuldenaar een groep vormen als bedoeld in artikel 24b van Boek 2 van het Burgerlijk Wetboek [...]."

45 Art. 372(1) DBA. *See e.g.* on Art. 372 DBA Menens (n 14) 495 *ff*; Pepels (n 7), Rob van den Sigtenhorst, Herstructurering groepsgaranties: mini-akkoord voor aansprakelijke groepsmaatschappijen (Art. 372 Fw), in Karen Harmsen and Michelle Reumers (eds), De WHOA van wet naar recht (Serie Recht en Praktijk) (Wolters Kluwer 2021).

(c) the relevant group company has either consented to the proposed amendment, or the creditor scheme is being offered by a restructuring expert (*herstructureringsdeskundige*);[46]
(d) the court would have (international) jurisdiction if the group company itself had offered a creditor scheme under the WHOA and applied for its approval itself;[47] and
(e) the relevant group company has not already offered a creditor scheme in respect of these obligations.[48]

Additionally,[49]
(f) the principal debtor (or restructuring expert) must supply all relevant 'scheme information' pursuant to Article 375 DBA also in relation to the non-debtor group companies, which includes, among other things, reorganization and liquidation valuations of the company;[50] and
(g) the court petitioned to confirm the scheme examines whether the scheme also complies with the confirmation requirements from Article 384 DBA in relation to those non-debtor group companies. This article most notably prescribes that non-consenting creditors or shareholders that are part of a non-consenting class may petition the court to deny confirmation of the creditor scheme if (i) they would be worse off under that scheme than they would be in case of a bankruptcy proceeding (the 'No Creditor Worse Off' or NCWO principle)[51] or if (ii) the legal ranking of rights of recourse is not maintained, prescribing that higher ranking classes creditors or shareholders should, in principle, be paid in full before other lower ranking classes receive any value (the 'Priority Rule').[52]

If these requirements are all met, a 'broad scheme' (or *breed akkoord*) may be offered and confirmed that also restructures creditors' rights arising out of group guarantees vis-à-vis non-debtor group companies, without the need to initiate separate proceedings concerning those group companies themselves.

---

46 The 'restructuring expert' is an independent court-appointed insolvency officer who, at the request of the debtor, any creditor, shareholder, the works council or staff representative, may be appointed by the court to prepare and submit a creditor scheme in the debtor's place. *See* Art. 371 DBA.

47 Which will often be the case. According to the Explanatory Memorandum, the mere circumstance that a foreign group company has guaranteed the debts of a principal debtor over which the Dutch court has jurisdiction may already be sufficient for the Dutch court to also declare itself competent to assume jurisdiction. It may also be sufficient that, when one or more creditor schemes are offered with respect to several group companies, one of those group companies has its COMI or an establishment in the Netherlands. *See Kamerstukken II* 2018/19, 35249 nr. 3, p. 42 (MvT). *See also* Pepels (n 7).

48 *Kamerstukken II* 2018/19, 35249 nr. 3, p. 42 (MvT).

49 Art. 372(2) DBA.

50 Art. 375(1)(d) and (e) in conjunction with Art. 372(2) DBA.

51 *See* 384(4)(c) and (d) DBA.

52 *See* 384(4)(b) DBA.

Considering the requirements for the application of Article 372 DBA, the WHOA conceptually treats the non-debtor group companies as if they were subject to Dutch Preventive Scheme proceedings themselves: the group companies need to be in financial distress themselves, the court must be allowed to assume jurisdiction to open Dutch Preventive Scheme proceedings in relation to them if they would have opened proceedings themselves, all relevant scheme information concerning them needs to be provided, and the creditor scheme also needs to comply with the confirmation requirements in relation to the relevant non-debtor group companies.[53] Importantly, and a valuable safety valve to prevent opportunistic discarding of guarantees, the application of the NCWO principle and Priority Rule ensures that creditors receive a payment on their guarantee under the broad scheme that does justice to the economic value of those guarantees. If, in addition to their payment from the debtor, they do not receive a payment on the guarantee that is at least equal to what they would have received in the bankruptcy of the relevant non-debtor group company and in line with their ranking within that bankruptcy proceeding, the court may deny confirmation of the Dutch Preventive Scheme.

Despite this conceptual approach, the WHOA does not treat the non-debtor group companies as actual subjects of the Dutch Preventive Scheme proceedings.[54] The WHOA qualifies the broad scheme as a *single* creditor scheme[55] offered by the debtor (and not also by the non-debtor group companies).[56] The obligations and rights imposed on debtors under the WHOA, e.g., to provide the relevant information[57] or to petition the court,[58] remain exclusively with the debtor (or the restructuring expert, where rele-

53 *See* Van den Sigtenhorst, who, as a result of this conceptual approach, states that, although a broad scheme as such is a single creditor scheme, Art. 372 DBA boils down to a *mini scheme* (or *mini-akkoord*) in relation to each individual non-debtor group company. *See* Van den Sigtenhorst (n 45).

54 It should be noted, however, that to the extent that the EU Insolvency Regulation (Regulation (EU) 2015/848 on insolvency proceedings) applies, case law of the Court of Justice of the European Union indicates that even where national law treats proceedings that relate to multiple debtors (or at least debts and assets of multiple legal entities) as a single insolvency proceeding (as is the case with a broad scheme), EU insolvency law, in principle, treats those debtors on an individual basis for purposes of determining jurisdiction, except where the Centre of Main Interest (or COMI) of those multiple debtors is located in the same Member State. *See, e.g.*, Case C-191/10, ECLI:EU:C:2011:838, *JOR* 2012/93, annotated by P.M. Veder, para. 13-29.

55 *See* Art. 372(1) DBA, which states that "a creditor scheme as mentioned in article 370, first subsection, can also prescribe the amendment of rights of creditors against [group companies]…." or in Dutch: "Een akkoord als bedoeld in artikel 370, eerste lid, kan ook voorzien in de wijziging van rechten van schuldeisers jegens [groepsmaatschappijen]…." (amendment and underlining SP).

56 *See* Art. 372(1)(d) DBA, which prescribes as a requirement that "the court has jurisdiction if these [group companies] would offer a creditor scheme pursuant to this section themselves and would file a request as mentioned in article 383, first subsection." or in Dutch "de rechtbank rechtsmacht heeft als deze [groepsmaatschappijen] zelf een akkoord op grond van deze afdeling zouden aanbieden en een verzoek zouden indienen als bedoeld in artikel 383, eerste lid." (amendment and underlining SP).

57 Art. 372(2)(a) DBA.

58 Art. 372(3) DBA.

vant). If a restructuring expert is appointed, non-debtor group companies are not even required to agree to the restructuring of their guarantees.[59]

The inclusion of provisions on group guarantee releases should be applauded as a welcome addition to the restructuring toolbox: they can halt the domino effect that the insolvency of group companies will often have. They will, however, only work in cases where the financial distress of the non-debtor group companies is merely the effect of the group guarantees having become due and payable due to the debtor's financial difficulties. The restructuring of the group guarantees alone should reinstate that group company as a financially healthy company. In cases where a full-fledged restructuring of obligations and/or a business reorganization is required (e.g., the sale of certain company divisions), Article 372 DBA will offer no relief.[60] The non-debtor group company would then have to engage in a separate restructuring itself.

5. Third-Party Releases Outside the Group and/or Outside the WHOA

5.1 *Limited to Group Companies?*

As is apparent from the foregoing, the WHOA allows for the release of non-debtor group company's guarantees under certain conditions. In relation to all other third-party guarantees, the WHOA prescribes that the regime of Article 160 DBA applies in Dutch Preventive Scheme proceedings.[61] Except for group guarantees in Dutch Preventive Scheme proceedings, the DBA thus prescribes a uniform approach for third-party releases in bankruptcy proceedings, suspension of payments proceedings and Dutch Preventive Scheme proceedings alike. Given the above described position of a majority of Dutch scholars on the nature of Dutch creditor schemes and (the rationale of) Article 160 DBA, i.e., that the release of third-party debt in a creditor scheme can only be imposed on *consenting* creditors, does that lead to the conclusion that Dutch law prohibits the imposition of third-party debt releases on non-consenting creditors in any type of (pre-)insolvency proceeding other than those releases exercised under Article 372 DBA?

---

59 Art. 372(1)(c) DBA.

60 *See* Art. 384(2)(e) DBA, pursuant to which a court must deny confirmation of the creditor scheme if its implementation is insufficiently certain, which could arguably be the case if the non-debtor group company's financial distress is not solved by the restructuring. Art. 384 DBA applies *m.m.* in respect of non-debtor group companies' guarantee restructurings under Art. 372 DBA, as follows from Art. 372(2)(b) DBA.

61 DBA, Art. 370(2). Informal translation: "If a third party, including a guarantor and co-obligor, is liable for a debt owed by the debtor to a creditor as referred to in the first paragraph or has provided security in any way for the payment of that debt, section 160 of the DBA shall apply mutatis mutandis, except insofar as it concerns an creditor scheme as referred to in section 372, first paragraph."

I would argue that there is a good case for 'not necessarily'.[62] First, when reading the Explanatory Note to Article 160 DBA, it is apparent that the legislator explicitly did not envisage that only consenting creditors could be bound to third-party release clauses.[63] During the legislative process concerning the DBA in the 1890s, various Members of the Dutch Parliament had proposed amending Article 160 DBA to include an automatic statutory release of third-party guarantees concerning creditors who voted in favour of the scheme. As is described in the Explanatory Note, they argued that it would be unreasonable if creditors who consented to a creditor scheme could still recover the remainder of their claims on a guarantor:

> "Art. 160. Concerning the system, prescribed by this article, the opinions [of Members of Parliament, addition SP] appeared divided. According to some the provision was not fair and should parties, that have voted in favor of the creditor scheme, not have any recourse on surety providers. These Members proposed to formulate [article 160 DBA, addition SP] as follows: "Unless the creditors have consented to the creditor scheme, they shall retain all their rights against the guarantors and co-obligors of the bankrupt debtor."[64]

The Dutch Government rejected that proposition and responded, among other things, that such a provision would wrongly incentivize creditors to vote against the scheme, even if the scheme itself would result in a higher distribution than they would receive in a liquidation of the debtor. As a result, it would harm the interest of the guarantors rather than improve it:

> "Against the provision proposed by the opponents of the article ["Unless the creditors have consented to the creditor scheme, they shall retain all their rights against the guarantors and co-obligors of the bankrupt debtor", addition SP], in addition to the objection raised in the report, could be argued that, in many cases, it will be more damaging to the guarantors and co-obligors. The creditor, in order not to lose his rights vis-à-vis the guarantors and co-obligors of the bankrupt, will then in any case have to vote against the creditor scheme, even though the creditors would gain more than in the event

62 *See* contrary Mennens (n 14) 520.

63 Bas Kortmann and Dennis Faber, Geschiedenis van de Faillissementswet, Heruitgave Van der Feltz, II (Wolters Kluwer 2016) 188-190.

64 Kortmann and Faber (n 63) 189. Informal translation. In Dutch: "Art. 160. Omtrent het stelsel, in dit artikel gevolgd, bleken de meeningen verdeeld. Volgens sommigen was de bepaling niet billijk en moisten zij, die vóór het akkoord hadden gestemd, geen verhaal hebben op de borgen. Deze leden wenschten het artikel aldus te formuleeren: "Tenzij de schuldeischers medegewerkt hebben tot het akkoord, behouden zij alle hunne rechten tegenover de borgen en medeschuldenaren van den gefailleerde"."

> of insolvency, to the detriment of those guarantors and co-obligors, who will then have to contribute more."[65]

It is thus clear that the Dutch legislator consciously and explicitly did not intend to include as a rule that only creditors who have voted in favour of a creditor scheme are bound to third-party release clauses included therein. Such a rule would undermine the purpose of the provision and could have a value destructive effect. As such, it appears difficult to maintain that pursuant to the general rules of contract law, creditors who have voted in favour of a creditor scheme are also bound by third-party releases included therein. The bankruptcy law *specialis* overrides the contract law *generalis*.

The question then becomes the following: should no, or all, creditors be bound? Admittedly, starting from the recent implementation of the WHOA, it is not obvious that the legislator intended to allow third-party releases in creditor schemes to extend beyond group guarantees in Dutch Preventive Scheme proceedings. The limitation of Article 372 DBA to group guarantees appears to be a deliberate choice. Prior drafts for the WHOA and its legislative predecessor (the *Wet Continuïteit Ondernemingen II*) both included third-party release mechanisms that were not limited to group guarantees but, for instance, also allowed a release of guarantees provided by a natural person who both owns and manages a company (a *directeur/grootaandeelhouder*, or *dga* in Dutch).[66] Mennens suggested that the legislator may have opted to limit the release mechanism of Article 372 DBA to group guarantees as it was only intended to prevent the above-described domino effect that may occur concerning distressed groups of companies and that may render the separate restructuring of individual group companies pointless.[67] Such problems are unlikely to arise when the liable third party is not a member of the same group of companies. The legislator thus appears to have seen insufficient reason to give Article 372 DBA a broader scope of application.

---

65 Kortmann and Faber (n 63) 190. Informal translation. In Dutch: "Tegen de door de bestrijders van het artikel voorgestelde bepaling ["Tenzij de schuldeischers medegewerkt hebben tot het akkoord, behouden zij all hunne rechten tegenover de borgen en medeschuldenaren van de gefailleerde", addition SP] geldt, behalve het bezwaar, in het Verslag aangevoerd, nog dit, dat het in vele gevallen de borgen en medeschuldenaren meer nadeel zal berokkenen. De schuldeischer zal dan, om zijne rechten tegenover de borgen en medeschuldenaren van den gefailleerde niet te verliezen, in ieder geval tegen het akkoord moeten stemmen, ook al zouden de schuldeischers daardoor meer erlangen, dan bij insolventie, en dit ten nadeele van die borgen en medeschuldenaren, die dan meer zullen moeten bijpassen."

66 *See* the Legislative Proposal (*Voorstel van Wet*) '*Wijziging van de Faillissementswet in verband met de invoering van de mogelijkheid tot het algemeen verbindend verklaren van een buiten faillissement gesloten akkoord ter herstructurering van de schulden (Wet continuïteit ondernemingen II)*', consultation version 14 August 2014, Art. 368(3) DBA and the Legislative Proposal (*Voorstel van Wet*) '*Wijziging van de Faillissementswet in verband met de invoering van de mogelijkheid tot homologatie van een onderhands akkoord om een dreigend faillissement af te wenden (Wet homologatie onderhands akkoord ter voorkoming van faillissement)*', consultation version 5 September 2017, Art. 370(2) DBA.

67 Mennens (n 14) 518.

The legislator's limited approach is also made explicit in the WHOA's explanatory note, where the legislator states in relation to Article 372 DBA:

> "**An exception to the rule that the scheme leaves rights to third parties unaffected is made for the case of an agreement as referred to in Article 372.** In such an arrangement, the intention is to include the restructuring of guarantees, insofar as these have been issued by companies that are part of the same group. **This can only be done if the conditions set out in that article are met.**"[68] (emphasis SP)

5.2 *Proposal for a More Tolerant Approach*

There are, however, various reasons to allow a broader, more tolerant approach to third-party releases. The first of these reasons concerns the dogmatic argument that a creditor scheme, as an agreement between the principal debtor involved in the proceedings and its creditors, can only amend their rights in relation to that specific debtor. Vriesendorp and Hermans had already argued at the beginning of the WHOA's legislative process that the principle exclusion of claims on third parties from the scope of the creditor scheme and its confirmation was somewhat artificial. If the majority of creditors similarly positioned vote in favour of the scheme, there is little difference between imposing third-party releases on creditors who have not voted in favour of the plan and imposing the other arrangements from the creditor scheme (e.g., release of 50 per cent of the claim against payment of the remaining 50 per cent).[69]

In his 2016 dissertation, Tollenaar similarly argued:

> "[...] If the majority of creditors with a claim against a particular third party agree to waive or modify their claim against the third party and the decision-making process is sound, I would not know of a good reason why the democratic decision-making process should be denied binding effect. The

68 Explanatory Note (*Memorie van Toelichting*) 'Wijziging van de Faillissementswet in verband met de invoering van de mogelijkheid tot homologatie van een onderhands akkoord om een dreigend faillissement af te wenden (Wet homologatie onderhands akkoord ter voorkoming van faillissement), consultatieversie 5 September 2017, p. 36. www.internetconsultatie.nl/wethomologatie. Informal translation. In Dutch: "Een uitzondering op de regel dat het akkoord rechten op derden onaangetast laat, wordt gemaakt voor het geval waarin sprake is van een akkoord als bedoeld in artikel 372. Bij een dergelijk akkoord is het de bedoeling om de herstructurering van garanties mee te nemen, voor zover die zijn afgegeven door vennootschappen die onderdeel vormen van dezelfde groep. Dit kan alleen als voldaan is aan de voorwaarden die in dat artikel zijn opgenomen."

69 Hermans en Vriesendorp (n 13) para. 4.a-b.

above principles regarding class voting and cram down can be applied mutatis mutandis to the restructuring of claims against third parties."[70]

In line with Vriesendorp, Hermans and Tollenaar, I see no real distinction between the imposition of the general provisions of a creditor scheme on creditors or the imposition of third-party release clauses on those same creditors. In both cases, the creditor scheme cannot rely on creditors' consent (*aanvaarding*) but would have to derive its binding power on creditors from the court's decision that confirms the scheme.[71] In both cases, arrangements that normally could not be imposed on creditors under regular contract law would become binding by virtue of the court's decision.[72]

With the enactment of the WHOA, the DBA now also explicitly stipulates that a creditor scheme can amend creditors' rights in relation to third parties under certain circumstances. To the extent that a creditor scheme in Dutch Preventive Scheme proceedings also includes a third-party release under Article 372 DBA, that release undeniably impacts the contractual arrangements between the non-debtor group company and the relevant creditor(s), whether they consented to the scheme or not. The dogmatic argument that a creditor scheme is an agreement between a debtor and its creditors and may thus only relate to the creditor-debtor relationship and the distribution of the debtor's estate appears no longer convincing with the enactment of the WHOA.[73]

A second argument in favour of a broader approach to third-party releases in creditor schemes lies within the main rationale behind Article 160 DBA. As the legislator

70 Informal translation. In Dutch: "[...] Indien de meerderheid van de crediteuren met een vordering op een bepaalde derde instemt met kwijtschelding of wijziging van hun vordering op de derde en de besluitvorming deugdelijk tot stand is gekomen, zou ik geen goede reden weten waarom aan de democratische besluitvorming bindende werking zou moeten worden onthouden. De bovenstaande principes ten aanzien van stemmen in klassen en cram down zijn mutatis mutandis toe te passen bij de herstructurering van vorderingen op derden." Differing from Hermans and Vriesendorp, Tollenaar argues that the relevant third party would have to comply with the same requirements as the main debtor, including the entry test concerning its (pre)insolvency ex Art. 370(1) DBA, *see* Tollenaar (n 18) 300-301.

71 An agreement under Dutch law requires an offer (*aanbod*) *and* the acceptance (*aanvaarding*) thereof. *See* Art. 6:217 Dutch Civil Code. *Cf.* Art. 3:300 Dutch Civil Code.

72 *Cf.* Aldous LJ in *British & Commonwealth Holdings Plc v. Barclays Bank Plc* in relation to the UK scheme of arrangements: "agreements which might be ultra vires and void become binding when approved by order of the court pursuant to section 425 of the Act of 1985." *See British & Commonwealth Holdings Plc v. Barclays Bank Plc* [1996] 1 W.L.R. 1 at 22; [1995] B.C.C. 1059 at [1078].

73 One could alternatively argue, building on Van den Sigtenhorst in n 45, that the section of the broad scheme that deals with the group guarantees conceptually qualifies as a 'mini scheme', a separate arrangement within the broad scheme. The 'mini scheme' could qualify as its own arrangement that only governs the relationship between the non-debtor group company and its creditors. If that reasoning would hold, the argument could be made that the broad scheme as such does not impact the contractual relationship between the non-debtor group company and its creditors, but the effect rather comes from the 'mini scheme', its own agreement. As discussed previously, however, the WHOA simply approaches the broad scheme as a single creditor scheme, offered by a single debtor (*e.g.* not *on behalf of* non-debtor group companies), that may even be offered without the consent of the relevant non-debtor group company in case a restructuring expert is appointed; *see* Art. 372(1)(c) DBA.

clarified in the Explanatory Note to the DBA, Article 160 DBA is intended to do justice to the economic function of guarantees. If the guarantor would be automatically released from its obligations as a result of a creditor scheme, the guarantee (or relevant other claim) would render it inoperative precisely at the time when that guarantee would be needed: when the debtor is unable to fulfil its obligations.[74] Moreover, as the legislator reasoned, a creditor scheme is intended not to dispose of rights but to assist creditors in attaining the maximum value on their claims and is a method of extrajudicial recovery.[75] The Explanatory Note to the WHOA similarly clarified the legislator's decision to apply the general rule from Article 160 DBA with the following example: if the debtor is granted a five-year stay of payment in the creditor scheme, without the reference to Article 160 DBA the due date for the claim against the guarantor would also shift by five years. The guarantee would then be rendered practically worthless.[76]

Although this rationale behind Article 160 DBA is rather convincing, it does not categorically prohibit third-party release clauses from being effectively included in creditor schemes. There would be no principle objection against such third-party effects, as long as the economic function of the relevant third-party debt (e.g. security for the original debt) would not be neglected and the release clause would assist creditors in attaining the maximum value on their claim. An automatic release of third-party debt (whether tort liability or a guarantee) by virtue of a creditor scheme without any explicit value contribution would obviously be contrary thereto. If, for instance, however, the relevant third party would make a contribution in relation to the released guarantees that reflects the economic value of the guarantee, or for that matter, a tort claim, there appears to be no reason to withhold such a release from being effective. The economic value of the relevant claim(s) would depend on the actual amount of those claim(s) but also on the extent to which the non-debtor party provides recovery for those claims.

If executed correctly, third-party release clauses could even be conducive to the legislator's intentions with Article 160 DBA. As Hermans and Vriesendorp have stated, a contribution by a third party (such as group companies, directors or insurers) to a creditor scheme against release of certain liabilities may very well result in the creditors receiving better – or at least quicker – payment on their claims.[77] It also contributes to the restructuring and reorganizational capabilities of both debtors and non-debtor parties alike by allowing simpler solutions for financial distress outside of formal insolvency proceedings, one of the legislator's overarching goals with the WHOA.[78]

---

74 Kortmann and Faber (n 63) 189. *See also* Veder and Thery (n 5) 266 and Wessels (n 18) para. 6161.
75 Kortmann and Faber (n 63) 189.
76 *Kamerstukken II* 2018/19, 35249 nr. 3, p. 35 (MvT).
77 Hermans en Vriesendorp (n 13) para. 4.
78 *Kamerstukken II* 2012/13, 29 911, nr. 74, p. 2.

In light of the foregoing, the rule embedded in Article 160 DBA could be seen as the default option, not the definitive outcome, and preventing the *automatic* release of certain third-party obligations but not third-party releases in general.

Tollenaar and Mennens have both argued that for any third-party release to be imposed on (non-consenting) creditors, the relevant third party would have to meet the same (pre-)insolvency entry test as the debtor.[79] The (pre-)insolvent state of the relevant party is the justification for deviating from the general principle of *pacta sunt servanda* and imposing the consenting majority's acceptance of a certain discount or otherwise amendment of the contractual arrangements on the non-consenting minority. As is apparent from Article 372 DBA, the Dutch legislator holds the same view: the non-debtor group company should be pre-insolvent, and the creditors should not be worse off than they would be in case of the non-debtor group company's bankruptcy and should receive a contribution in accordance with the Priority Rule.[80]

Instead of limiting the application of third-party releases to pre-insolvent non-debtor parties, one could also refer to the aforementioned principle that third-party releases would require a value contribution that reflects the economic value of the relevant claim(s). By doing so, a similar result would be attained. A contribution that reflects less than the full amount of the relevant claim(s) would only be allowed if the non-debtor party would have insufficient assets to repay the relevant claims in full.

As opposed to requiring (pre-)insolvency, however, this value contribution test would simultaneously provide for a more broadly applicable and efficient mechanism to release non-debtor liabilities in creditor schemes. Third-party releases in creditor schemes could then not only be applied to prevent (imminent) insolvency of the relevant non-debtor parties but would also allow for an effective mechanism within the already existing collective preventive or court supervised formal insolvency proceeding to settle claims that relate to the debtor's (pre-)insolvency, but are owed by other, solvent non-debtor parties (such as shareholders, directors and/or their insurers).

5.3 *A Tolerant Approach Would Fit Existing Case Law*

While scholars have particularly referenced the aforementioned *De Maes Janssens* judgment[81] to argue that a creditor scheme cannot alter or waive claims of non-consenting creditors on non-debtor parties, that case would actually fit this more tolerant framework. Rather than understanding it as a general prohibition on any form of third-party

79 *See* Tollenaar (n 18) 300-301 and Mennens (n 14) 498-499 and the references to other parts of their dissertations included there. *See also* Veder and Thery and their substantiation as to why they only consider upstream guarantees, Veder and Thery (n 5) 263.

80 *See* Art. 372(1)(b) in conjunction with Art. 370(1) DBA.

81 *See supra* n 27.

effect to creditor schemes, it could also be understood to only prevent *automatic* release of third parties.

In that matter, the relevant creditor (Credit Lyonnais Bank Nederland N.V., the **Bank**) had consented to a creditor scheme offered in the bankruptcy proceeding concerning the husband of Mrs. De Maes Janssens, pursuant to which the Bank would receive a payment of 35 cents on the *Gulden*. Mrs. De Maes Janssens, the third-party debtor in that case, argued that as the Bank had consented to the creditor scheme, it could no longer claim any damages (the remaining 65 per cent of its claim) on the basis of Dutch tort law.[82]

If the Dutch Supreme Court had ruled in favour of Mrs. De Maes Janssens, she would have automatically been released from any potential tort liability and benefited from the creditor scheme without having made any payment in that regard or without the scheme even stipulating a release of claims against her. The Dutch Supreme Court rightfully reasoned that would be contrary to the rationale behind Article 160 DBA. That would not have done justice to the economic value of the Bank's claim on Mrs. De Maes Janssens.

But what if the Bank had received an additional payment that is reflective of the value of its claim on Mrs. De Maes Janssens? If, for instance, she had had insufficient assets to repay the remaining 65 per cent to the Bank, taking her total estate into account, it would have been reasonable to allow a discount on the payment that reflects the relevant deficit. If her estate had been sufficient to repay the bank in full and there was no reason why the Bank's claim on her was actually less than the remaining 65 per cent of the Bank's original claim, Article 160 DBA (and the ratio behind it) would have prescribed full payment of that remaining amount.

Case law on the WHOA's mechanism of dealing with third-party debt[83] also indicates that the more tolerant approach advocated in this report is not completely made out of thin air. In one of those cases, the District Court of Middle-Netherlands made an *obiter dictum* in relation to third-party releases outside the scope of Article 372 DBA. The District Court starts off by stating that it is uncertain whether such third-party releases are possible under the WHOA:

> "In addition, [company 1], in addition to other parties, will receive a final discharge in the creditors composition of potential claims from other creditors.

82 Art. 6:162 ff Dutch Civil Code.

83 *See* for cases on Art. 372 DBA and on other types of third-party release clauses: District Court of Amsterdam 5 August 2021, *JOR* 2022/102, m. nt. R. van den Sigtenhorst and in the same restructuring District Court of Amsterdam 15 February 2021, *JOR* 2022/100, m. nt. M.M. Hoving; District Court of Limburg 8 October 2021, *JOR* 2022/20, m. nt. Tekstra; District Court Middle-Netherlands, 10 November 2021, *JOR* 2022/21, m. nt. N.B. Pannevis.

> It is questionable whether that is possible, but the answer to this question is irrelevant to the outcome of this case. […]."[84]

The judgment, however, continues in a way that – to the open-minded reader – could be understood as a hint in favour of third-party releases outside the scope of Article 372 DBA, if the value attributed to that release and the particular position of the creditors vis-à-vis the non-debtor party are sufficiently accounted for:

> "[…] However, insofar as such a discharge is permitted, the value of this final discharge is not included in the determination of the liquidation value and the possible claims of creditors against [company 1] are not further explained in the plan."[85]

As is also apparent from this excerpt of the judgment, the advocated more tolerant approach to third-party releases does presume that the relevant creditors are enabled to make an informed and individual decision on the release. As part of the scheme information, those creditors should thus be provided with the required information (a valuation of the non-debtor, descriptions of the relevant claims and the impact of the creditor scheme thereon) to determine whether the contributed value reflects the economic value of the third-party debt. Similar to Article 372 DBA,[86] it would be sensible to impose the obligation to provide such information on the party proposing the creditor scheme. If insufficient information is provided, the court could, for example, defer its decision on the confirmation (*aanhouden*) and grant the opportunity to file additional information[87] or deny confirmation of the creditor scheme.[88]

---

84 District Court Middle-Netherlands, 10 November 2021, *JOR* 2022/21, m. nt. N.B. Pannevis, para. 5.10. Informal translation. In Dutch: "Daar komt bij dat [onderneming 1], naast andere partijen, in het akkoord een finale kwijting ontvangt van eventuele aanspraken van andere schuldeisers. Het is de vraag of dat mogelijk is, maar het antwoord op deze vraag is niet van belang voor de uitkomst in deze zaak. […]."

85 *Ibid.* Informal translation. In Dutch: "[…] Voor zover echter een dergelijke kwijting is toegestaan, geldt dat de waarde van deze finale kwijting niet is meegenomen bij bepaling van de liquidatiewaarde en de mogelijke aanspraken van schuldeisers jegens [onderneming 1] zijn in het akkoord niet verder toegelicht."

86 Art. 372(2)(a) DBA.

87 *See, e.g.*, for a recent matter concerning a Dutch suspension of payments proceeding where the judgment was deferred and the administrator was granted an additional term to further investigate the value of certain assets if confirmation was denied and the company would have gone bankrupt: District Court Middle-Netherlands, 3 August 2021, *JOR* 2022/15, m. nt. E.F. Groot.

88 On the basis of Art. 153(3), in case of bankruptcy, Art. 272(3) in case of suspension of payments or Art. 384(2)(i) DBA in case of a Dutch Preventive Scheme proceeding.

5.4 A More Tolerant Approach, but Where Do We Draw the Line?

The final query then remains, assuming such a broad application of third-party releases, which third-party liabilities are eligible to be released via a creditor scheme, i.e., where do we draw the line?

In determining whether certain third-party release clauses included in English schemes of arrangement were admissible, English courts have used the phrase: "[...] a scheme which varies or releases creditors' claims against the company on terms which require them to bring into account and release **rights of action against third parties designed to recover the same loss** [...]"[89] And, similarly, "... **rights of action [that] are designed to recover the same loss as arises from the scheme creditors' claims against the company**...."[90] Among other things, they have also taken into account that payment on the relevant third-party obligation "would have resulted in a reduction of the scheme creditors' claims against the company".[91]

Taking inspiration from this English case law, it could be proposed that a third-party release clause included in a Dutch creditor scheme can effectively be imposed on creditors only if their claims on the non-debtor parties are claims that concern the recovery of the loss that they incurred as a result of the debtor's non-payment (i.e., a claim on a non-debtor party that is the direct result of their claim on the debtor remaining unpaid). Effectively, if the non-debtor party had paid those obligations, that would have resulted in a reduction of the scheme creditors' claims against the debtor (and *vice versa*).

That threshold would obviously generally be met in relation to corporate guarantees for the debtor's obligations by group companies, directors, shareholders or other third parties (referred to in paragraph 2 as Category 1).

Where the relevant third-party debt concerns tort liabilities of (*de facto*) directors or shareholders (or their insurers) in relation to their involvement with the debtor prior to its insolvency (Category 2 in paragraph 2), that will often also be the case if those liabilities relate to the fact that the debtor does not provide sufficient recourse for its creditors, and/or its assets were unlawfully transferred prior to the proceedings (e.g., directors' or shareholders' liability based on the *Ontvanger/Roelofsen* formula or relating to unlawfully received dividend).

The release of claims against decision makers and/or advisors involved in a restructuring or insolvency process, such as directors or bankruptcy trustees (Category 3), may require a more thorough analysis, to the extent that those claims relate to actions in the execution of the restructuring or even post-restructuring. As Mennens has

89 *Re Lehman Brothers* [2009] EWCA Civ 1161; [2010] B.C.C. 272 at [63].
90 *Re La Seda* [2010] EWHC 1364 (Ch); [2011] 1 B.C.L.C. 555 at [21].
91 *Re La Seda* [2010] EWHC 1364 (Ch); [2011] 1 B.C.L.C. 555 at [22].

argued, minimizing the reluctance of advisors and decision makers to expose themselves to certain risks in large restructurings (and thus not taking optimal decisions) is, first and foremost, a matter of ensuring that the liability threshold for these parties reflects that risk, rather than a question of whether or not waivers of such claims via a third-party release in a creditor scheme are admissible.[92] It could be argued that liability in relation to the execution of the restructuring does not concern the recovery of the loss that arises from the debtor's unpaid debts but, rather, of the execution of the creditor scheme.[93]

In itself, however, creditor schemes will be the result of debtors' inability to meet their obligations (now or in the near future). And, if the release is deemed a precondition for the decision makers' and/or advisors' involvement in the restructuring, the economic value would arguably equal the value realized with the scheme. Moreover, by voting in majority in favour of the creditor scheme, the creditors will have also voted in support of the actions that have led to the development of that scheme and the subsequent envisaged actions for the implementation thereof.[94] While there is something to be said for both sides, there would be a strong case in favour of allowing third-party releases in relation to decision makers and/or advisors.

6. CONCLUSION

A majority of Dutch scholars that have written on this topic have long assumed that a creditor scheme, being an agreement between a debtor and its creditors, cannot effectively impose third-party release clauses on creditors that have not voted in favour of the scheme. Such third-party release clauses were deemed 'extraneous scheme provisions' and, as such, outside the scope of the court's confirmation of the scheme. Only creditors that consent to a creditor scheme could be bound by third-party releases, on the basis of general contracting law (they accepted the offer to also amend certain third-party debt).

As has been outlined in the foregoing, there are, however, several arguments in favour of a more tolerant view of third-party release clauses in Dutch creditor schemes.

92 Mennens (n 14) 520.

93 Mennens mentions in relation to the English Scheme of Arrangements that payment by any of these parties would generally not reduce the total outstanding debt of the debtor and therefore questions the validity of such releases but also states that release clauses in relation to advisors, directors and insolvency practitioners in scheme documentation are common practice and appear to be uncontested. *See* Mennens (n 14) 503-504.

94 That would be different in relation to liability for actions concerning the subsequent implementation of the creditor scheme that are not provided for in the scheme or for fraudulent actions. A release of claims against decision makers and/or advisors involved in a restructuring or insolvency process could, as such, easily be compared with the Dutch practice of discharge (*décharge*) by the Shareholders' Meeting of the Members of the Board from their liabilities.

First, the principle that only creditors that have voted in favour of the plan are bound by such extraneous scheme provisions is directly contrary to the intentions of the Dutch legislator; it would wrongly incentive creditors to vote against a creditor scheme, even where that scheme would result in a higher payment than they would receive in a liquidation scenario. In turn, that would harm the relevant third party, who would be confronted with a higher claim than it would be if the creditor scheme had been adopted and confirmed.

Second, with the recent implementation of the WHOA in the DBA, the dogmatic argument that a creditor scheme, being an agreement between the debtor and its creditors, can only amend rights in those relationships (absent explicit consent thereto) has become significantly less convincing. The WHOA explicitly offers the possibility of third-party releases, albeit only in the context of group guarantees.

Approaching it from a more positive perspective, if sufficient safeguards are taken into account, the permission of third-party releases outside the context of group guarantees in Dutch Preventive Scheme proceedings could actually benefit creditors. As long as the economic value of the relevant third-party obligation is taken into consideration, it could very well result in creditors receiving more, or at least quicker, payment on their claims. Additionally, it would be conducive to the restructuring capabilities of both debtors and non-debtors alike.

All in all, the time may very well have come to re-evaluate the Dutch stance on third-party releases in creditor schemes. Recent Dutch case law on the WHOA could be understood as a hint that the judges of the WHOA pool are considering doing just that.[95]

95 The (near) future will have to prove whether it was a bad idea to extrapolate an *obiter dictum* to a prediction or whether Dutch court will, indeed, allow a more tolerant approach to third-party releases.

Settling Mass Damage Claims Inside and Outside Insolvency Procedures: A Comparison of the Available Procedures

Ruud Hermans[*]

1. Introduction

Lindsey Simon and Ralph Brubaker have given a fascinating presentation on the boundaries of settling mass damage claims in bankruptcy in the United States. American practice shows that there is a tendency to use insolvency law to settle mass damages claims. Clearly, debtors are exploring the limits of what is possible. In my opinion, in order to protect the interests of the injured parties, it will be necessary, and unavoidable, that either the legislature or the judiciary will have to set limits on what is allowed in this respect.

In the Netherlands we are not that far yet. There are examples of mass damage claims that have been settled through an insolvency procedure, such as the recent Steinhoff securities claim.[1] The reasoning behind this is, however, still in its infancy. NACIIL has requested me to share my thoughts with you on the possibilities of settling mass damage claims in Dutch insolvency procedures through a confirmed restructuring plan. The insolvency procedures I will discuss are bankruptcy, suspension of payments and Court confirmation of an Extrajudicial Restructuring Plan (the Dutch Preventive Scheme, also known as the WHOA). I will compare these settlement options with the possibility of offering an opt-out settlement outside of insolvency, which is possible under the Dutch Act on the Collective Settlement of Mass Damage Claims (known as the WCAM or Mass Damage Settlement Act) and the Resolution of Mass Damage in Collective Action Act (known as the WAMCA). I will not deal separately with the settlement option offered by the WAMCA, because Article 1018h(2) Dutch Code of Civil

* Fellow, Radboud Business Law Institute, Radboud University Nijmegen; substitute judge The Hague Court of Appeal. This report was presented at the NACIIL annual meeting on 16 June 2022, and the written version was finalized in October 2022.

1 District Court Amsterdam 23 September 2021, ECLI:NL:RBAMS:2021:5452, *JOR* 2022/17, annotation R.J. van Galen.

Procedure (DCCP) declares the provisions of the Mass Damage Settlement Act to be applicable on such a settlement mutatis mutandis.

Common to these procedures is the fact that mass damage claims of a large group of creditors against a debtor are settled bindingly in a collective agreement, without the need for the creditors to agree to this settlement individually. However, there are also major differences. As a result of those differences, in many cases not every type of collective procedure is available to settle every mass damage claim. Nevertheless, there are also situations where several procedures can be used. In those situations parties can choose the type of collective procedure that suits them best.

In the following, I will first outline the similarities and differences between the different procedures. Secondly, I will give an example of a mass damage claim that has been settled through a bankruptcy procedure and discuss whether that mass damage claim could also have been settled through an opt-out settlement. I will conclude with a few remarks on the lessons that can be drawn from this overview.

A preliminary remark may be noted. The Mass Damage Settlement Act can also be used by a bankruptcy receiver to settle mass damages claims with the injured parties. The legislator has created this option in order to give the receivers in the bankruptcy of DSB Bank the opportunity to settle ten thousand duty-of-care claims with DSB borrowers.[2] For want of time, I will not go into this matter any further.

2. Insolvency Requirement

Bankruptcy procedures can only be initiated when the insolvency criteria are met. These insolvency criteria differ within the various insolvency procedures provided for in the Dutch Bankruptcy Act (DBA):

- Bankruptcy: the debtor is in the state of having ceased to pay (Art. 1(1) DBA);
- Suspension of payments: the debtor foresees that he cannot continue to pay his due debts (Art. 214(1) DBA);
- Dutch Preventive Scheme: the debtor is in a situation where it is reasonably likely that he will not be able to continue paying his debts (Art. 370(1) DBA).

For the use of the Mass Damage Settlement Act there is, of course, no insolvency requirement.

2 Amsterdam Court of Appeal 12 November 2013, ECLI:NL:GHAMS:2013:3918, *JOR* 2013/343, annotation A.F.J.A. Leijten; Amsterdam Court of Appeal 13 May 2014, ECLI:NL:GHAMS:2014:1690, *JOR* 2015/9; Amsterdam Court of Appeal 4 November 2014, ECLI:NL:GHAMS:2014:4560, *JOR* 2015/10, annotation I.N. Tzankova.

3. Debts That Can Be Involved in a Collective Settlement

A confirmed restructuring plan in an insolvency procedure is not binding on all types of creditors. Only some types of creditors can be bound by the plan against their will. In addition, this also differs per type of insolvency procedure. Article 157 DBA respectively Article 273 DBA provides that a restructuring plan is binding on all non-priority creditors. As tort victims are non-priority creditors, their claims can be compromised in a confirmed restructuring plan in a bankruptcy or suspension of payment procedure.

Article 385 DBA provides that the confirmed Dutch Preventive Scheme is binding on the debtor and all voting creditors. In a Dutch Preventive Scheme the creditors are divided into classes, and each class affected by the scheme can vote. Tort victims will most likely form a separate class and can be compromised.

In all types of insolvency procedures, it must be established who is a creditor. The fixation principle enshrined in Article 24 of the DBA means that, in principle, the estate is not liable for debts arising after the declaration of bankruptcy. 'In principle', because there are exceptions. I will come back to those exceptions later. A settlement agreement, whether it is offered in bankruptcy, suspension of payments or in a Dutch Preventive Scheme, can only apply to debts to 'creditors'. Therefore, as a starting point, this applies to debts that exist at the time of the opening of the insolvency procedure.

The question therefore arises as to when a claim exists. A distinction can be made between claims arising from contracts and claims arising from torts. To keep it simple, I will only discuss the moment of tort claims coming into existence. The starting point is that a claim comes into existence when all the conditions of Article 6:162 Dutch Civil Code (DCC) (the general provision on tortious liability) are met: not only must the unlawful act have taken place, but the damage must also have been suffered.

The determination of whether or a tort claim exists is rather straightforward in those situations where a one-time event directly causes damage. For example, damages suffered by shareholders because the debtor did not timely disclose price sensitive information.

It becomes more complicated when the event has taken place before the opening of the insolvency procedure and the loss partly arose before the opening, but also partly thereafter. For example, income foregone by the victim of treatment with a defective drug for the rest of his or her working life, when the treatment took place before the opening of the insolvency procedure but the expected retirement date of the victim is decades thereafter. Can, then, the loss, also insofar as it occurred after the opening of the insolvency procedure, be included in the restructuring plan?

A third possibility is that the loss-causing event occurred prior to insolvency but it is still uncertain whether damage will be incurred. As an example I mention the situation of exposure to asbestos. Given the long incubation period between the exposure and the occurrence of asbestos-related illnesses, it is unclear whether the victim will become sick and suffer damage. Can that damage be resolved in the restructuring plan?

A fourth possibility is the situation of creeping damage: the damage-causing event occurred before insolvency and continues thereafter, as could be the case with environmental pollution. Again, the question arises whether the restructuring plan can deal with those claims.

Time is too short to go into this in depth. In part, Articles 129-133 DBA, which deal with the valuation of non-payable receivables or receivables subject to a condition precedent offer a solution. Furthermore, one can argue that tort claims that have their origin in a legal relationship that existed before the opening of the insolvency proceedings can be treated as receivables in insolvency, as the Supreme Court ruled in the *Koot Beheer/Tideman* and *Credit Suisse/Jongepier* cases regarding claims arising from contract.[3] In my opinion, this line of cases can be extended to claims arising out of tort. But even if the concept of an existing creditor is interpreted extensively, a settlement agreement can only be used to bind creditors holding claims existing on or having their origin in a legal relationship that existed before the opening of the insolvency procedure.

The limitation that only existing mass damage claims can be dealt with in a restructuring plan does not apply to a collective settlement that is declared binding on the basis of the Mass Damage Settlement Act. Article 7:907(1) DCC provides that the settlement must be concluded for the purpose of compensation for damage caused by an event or similar events. This does not exclude compensation for future damage, i.e. damage incurred after the entering into the collective settlement agreement caused by previous events. There is, of course, a limitation. After the collective settlement agreement has been declared binding, those entitled to compensation may opt out of the settlement. Parties whose claims arise after the opt-out period expires, typically 3 to 6 months after the court order confirming the settlement agreement, cannot be expected to opt out, because they were unaware that they had a claim covered by the settlement agreement. The nature of the Mass Damage Settlement Act implies that those creditors cannot be bound by the collective settlement agreement.

4. THE CONTENT OF THE COLLECTIVE SETTLEMENT AGREEMENT OR RESTRUCTURING PLAN

Experience shows that legal practitioners are creative in shaping collective settlement agreements and restructuring plans. The starting point for both a restructuring plan in insolvency and a collective settlement agreement is the principle of freedom of contract. The mandatory requirements for such plans and agreements in the Bankruptcy Act and

3 Supreme Court 19 April 2013, ECLI:NL:HR:2013:BY6108, *NJ* 2013/291, annotation F.J.M. Verstijlen, *JOR* 2013/224, annotation G.A.J. Boekraad (*Koot Beheer/Tideman qq*); Supreme Court 23 March 2018, ECLI:NL:HR:2018:424, *NJ* 2018/290. annotation F.J.M. Verstijlen, *JOR* 2018/254, annotation N.S.G.J. Vermunt and N.E.D. Faber (*Credit Suisse/Jongepier qq*).

the Civil Code can easily be dealt with. However, in all proceedings the Court can refuse to confirm the restructuring plan or refuse to declare the collective settlement agreement binding if the plan or agreement is not considered to be fair and equitable. For this reason, the confirmation requirements do impose restrictions on the content of the collective settlement.

An interesting question is to what extent the settlement can also contain a third-party clause in which the creditors waive their claims against third parties. I refer to Pepels' article, which addresses this topic in depth.

5. Involvement of Creditors in the Formation of the Settlement Agreement

A restructuring plan in an insolvency procedure must be accepted by a qualified majority of creditors. In bankruptcy proceedings and suspension of payments proceedings, all non-priority creditors can vote on the proposed restructuring plan, including creditors who do not have a mass tort claim. Required is the consent of the majority of the creditors appearing at the meeting, representing at least half of the number of the non-priority claims (Art. 145 DBA; Art. 268 DBA).

In the case of suspension of payment, an exception is possible if there are more than 5,000 creditors. In that case, the court may appoint a committee of representation of at least nine members who can vote on the agreement, instead of the creditors themselves (Arts. 281b et seq. DBA). Recently, this provision was applied in the suspension of payment granted to Steinhoff and to DSB.[4]

In a Dutch Preventive Scheme (WHOA) the creditors are divided into classes, and each class affected by the scheme can vote. Tort victims will most likely form a separate class. Article 381(7) DBA provides that a class of creditors has consented to the agreement if the decision to consent has been made by a group of creditors who together represent at least two-thirds of the total amount of claims belonging to the creditors who voted within that class. This seems to give the tort victims a decisive vote on a proposed settlement agreement. However, Article 384(4) DBA gives the Court the power to confirm a plan over the objection of a class, if there is at least one consenting class, the so-called cross class cram down. So there is, at least in theory, a possibility that tort victims can be bound by a settlement rejected by a majority of them, but it is hard to imagine that a judge would actually use such cram down powers against the vote of the

4 District Court Amsterdam 28 May 2021, ECLI:NL:RBAMS:2021:3197, *JOR* 2021/280, annotation R.J. van Galen; District Court Amsterdam 9 March 2022, https://content.dsb.nl/publications/29/2022.03.09%20-%20Publicatie%20Rechtbank%20-%20Beschikking%20toewijzing%20verzoek%20benoeming%20commissie%20van%20vertegenwoordiging.pdf.

tort claimants as a class, in case the debtor's financial problems are clearly mass tort related.

A collective settlement outside insolvency is entered into by a not-for-profit claim organization on behalf of the injured parties. The injured parties themselves do not have voting rights, but they may opt out of the settlement. Furthermore, the not-for-profit claim organization should be representative of the injured parties, and its board members may not themselves have a financial interest in the settlement.

6. Criterion for Confirmation of the Restructuring plan or Declaring the Collective Settlement Binding

In all situations, the agreement (i.e. the restructuring plan or the collective settlement) must be court approved (i.e. confirmed or declared binding). However, the criterion for approval of the agreement differs in the various procedures. In all proceedings, there are a number of mandatory grounds for refusing confirmation. These relate to the way in which the agreement was concluded or to the certainty that the debtor can actually fulfil its obligations. In all proceedings, the court can also refuse to confirm the agreement ex officio.

In insolvency procedures, the judge will assess, among other elements, whether the distribution to the creditors according to the agreement is higher than a distribution would have been in bankruptcy (the 'no creditor worse off' test). In an opt-out collective settlement, the court will refuse confirmation if the compensation for the injured is not fair and equitable.

An important difference between confirmation of the restructuring plan in insolvency procedures and approval of an opt-out collective settlement is the possibility to amend the content of the agreement, in order to accommodate concerns of the court. In insolvency proceedings this is not possible. After the vote, the agreement cannot be changed. Furthermore, in an insolvency procedure a restructuring plan can only be offered once. However, during the confirmation procedure of a collective settlement agreement, the court can suggest that parties amend the collective settlement. This is what the court did in both the Fortis and the DSB collective settlements.[5]

5 Amsterdam Court of Appeal 13 May 2014, ECLI:NL:GHAMS:2014:1690, *JOR* 2015/9 (*DSB*); Amsterdam Court of Appeal 16 June 2017, ECLI:NL:GHAMS:2017:2257, Amsterdam Court of Appeal 5 February 2018, ECLI:NL:GHAMS:2018:368 (*Fortis*).

7. Finality

A confirmed agreement provides finality for the debtor. All creditors are bound by the contents of the agreement that amend their rights. This is not the case with a collective settlement agreement that has been declared binding. In that case, the aggrieved parties have the opportunity to make an opt-out declaration. If a large number of creditors do so, the debtor has not yet resolved the dispute. In the nine collective settlements that have been approved so far, only in the Dexia settlement have there been many opt-outs, namely 23,947. That is in itself a large number. In relative numbers, more than 90% of the injured parties have not done so. In practice, even a binding collective settlement does provide finality to the debtor, at least to a very large extent.

8. Deal Certainty

Every debtor will want to have as much certainty as possible that the deal he is offering will be accepted and confirmed. In an insolvency procedure there are two uncertainties: Firstly, will the creditors vote for the restructuring plan, and, secondly, will the court confirm it? A key risk factor is especially that creditors with small claims can torpedo an agreement supported by the creditors with large claims. In the case of a collective settlement, there is a risk that the court may suggest that the parties amend the collective settlement agreement. In practice, this means that the debtor is more or less forced to agree to an improved settlement agreement, which is more costly. The risk hereof is perceived as high. After the Fortis and the DSB collective settlements, in which the court 'forced' Fortis and the DSB receivers to improve their offer, no further requests have been submitted to declare a collective settlement binding.

9. Costs and Duration of Proceedings

The turnaround time of an insolvency procedure if a settlement is offered can be very short. A Dutch Preventive Scheme procedure can be completed in 2 to 3 months. A suspension of payments procedure can also be completed within this time frame if the restructuring plan is offered at the same time as the request for suspension of payments is filled. In contrast, the procedure to declare a collective settlement binding (including the opt-out period) takes 1 to 2 years.

The cost of insolvency proceedings in which a restructuring plan is offered can be significantly lower than the costs of getting an opt-out collective settlement approved. However, this depends heavily on the circumstances of the case. In general, one cannot say which procedure is more expensive.

10. Debtor in Possession

After the opening of a bankruptcy proceeding and a suspension of payments procedure, the court appoints an insolvency practitioner, which implies the debtor's board losing control. This is a high price to be paid to use a bankruptcy procedure to restructure a mass damage claim. The Dutch Preventive Scheme is much more attractive in this respect, as it is a debtor in possession procedure. Also, in case of an opt-out collective settlement the debtor remains, of course, in control.

11. Examples of Mass Damage Claims Resolved through Insolvency Proceedings

The most notable example of an insolvency procedure to resolve a mass damage claim in the Netherlands is the Steinhoff case. Steinhoff filed for suspension of payments in January 2021 and simultaneously filed a draft restructuring plan. As there were more than 5,000 creditors, the court appointed a committee of representation to vote on the plan. Because Steinhoff was a holding company without any operating activities, losing control to an insolvency practitioner was not considered to be a major obstacle. Apparently, Steinhoff weighed the pros and cons of opt-out settlement agreement and a Dutch Preventive Scheme and decided that a suspension of payments procedure served its objectives best.

12. Conclusion

To sum up, mass damage claims can, depending on the circumstances of the case, be bindingly resolved in an insolvency procedure if the debtor fulfils the insolvency criterium required for the opening of the desired insolvency procedure. Alternatively, the debtor can use the Mass Damages Settlement Act assuming he can conclude a collective settlement agreement with a claim organization that is representative of the injured parties. Each possible procedure to resolve the mass damage claim has its pros and cons. In my view, in case of insolvency of the debtor, the Dutch Preventive Scheme is best suited to dealing with mass damage claims. This is because, firstly, it is a debtor in possession procedure, which is in the interest of the debtor, and, secondly, because injured parties can vote as a separate class on the proposed plan, which is in the interest of the injured parties. Whether the Dutch Preventive Scheme will be used for this purpose remains to be seen. Debtors might be reluctant to use the Dutch Preventive Scheme for several reasons. One reason might be a lack of successful precedents. Another reason might be lack of clarity as to which claims can be resolved in a restructuring plan.

www.ingramcontent.com/pod-product-compliance
Lightning Source LLC
Chambersburg PA
CBHW061356240926
51846CB00007B/1430
* 9 7 8 9 0 4 7 3 0 1 6 8 4 *